Maria Lives!

Woman of Courage and Vision

Maria Lebt!

Frau mit Mut und Weitsicht

Written in English and German

by
Marianne Tong

To my three daughters who are
fearlessly following in the footsteps
of their many grandmothers

circa 1908

Maria Hammes

Granddaughter of Maria Korzilius

Grandmother of the author, Marianne Tong

Foreword

The document arrived as an e-mail attachment from my cousin in Germany. I barely had time to notice the name of my great-grandfather, Moritz Hammes, at the top of the page, so I printed out the document to go over carefully later that day.

As I sat down that evening with a cool drink, I read through all the vital statistics about the common ancestry my cousin had discovered in the regional archives. The records of several generations only showed names and dates of birth, marriage and death. Not much else. Most of these folks had lived in the village of Macken in the Hunsrück Mountains, where the sturdy homestead stood unfazed through many trials and tribulations. After World War II, my grandmother had escaped the bombed-out city of Koblenz and returned to this ancestral home where she was able to take care of me. My mother remained in the city, moving from home to home among her surviving friends, sewing and mending clothes. As I was reading the cold unfeeling document, my mind drifted back to those five wonderful years I spent in the same cozy house.

Suddenly my pleasant musings were interrupted by a shocking statistic. No explanation! Just the simple facts stared back at me from the page. As a mother, I was stunned. I could only imagine what my great-great-grandmother must have gone through. How did she have the courage to raise children? My memories of that ancestral village combined with my imagination, so I began to construct a story from those stark statistics.

Vorwort

Ich erhielt das Dokument als E-mail Anhang von meiner Kusine in Deutschland. Ich hatte kaum Zeit den Namen meines Urgrossvaters, Moritz Hammes, zu lesen. Deshalb druckte ich die Auszüge um sie später besser zu untersuchen.

Als ich mich abends mit einen Getränk gemütlich niederließ, konnte ich die gesamten statistische Dateien über meine Vorahnen gründlich durchlesen. Die Information von den Generationen gab weiter nichts als die Namen, Geburts- Hochzeit- und Todestage der Personen. Die Mehrzahl unserer Familie wohnten in Macken im Hunsrück, wo das alte Wohnhaus viel Freude und Elend überlebte. Nach dem zweiten Weltkrieg, flüchtete meine Grossmutter aus dem bombenzerstörten Koblenz zurück zu ihrem Geburtsort. Meine Mutter blieb in der Stadt. Weil sie Schneiderin war, zog sie von einer Freundin zur Anderen, um deren Kleidung zu verbessern. Während dem Lesen, wehten Erinnerungen um meinen Kopf. Ich dachte zurück an die wunderbaren Jahre, die ich im selben Haus in Macken verbrachte.

Plötzlich wurden meine angenehmen Gedanken von einem Schock unterbrochen. Keine Erklärung! Bloss die kalten Dateien standen auf dem Blatt Papier. Als Mutter war ich sprachlos. Ich konnte mir kaum vorstellen, was meine Ururgrossmutter erlebt haben muss. Woher bekam sie den Mut Kinder auf die Welt zu setzen? Meine eigenen Erinnerungen an das Dorf meiner Vorahnen vermischten sich mit meiner Einbildungskraft, und so fing ich eine Geschichte von den nackten Statistiken zu konstruieren an.

When I told my uncle in Germany about my story, he wanted to read it in German. I promised that I would translate it and send him a copy. Earlier I had written a story about Macken, "The Healing Village" in English This story was published as part of my memoir, _The Little Girl That Could._ I also translated this story and sent it to my uncle and a childhood friend.

In _Maria Lives!_, I'm publishing both my English and German versions of the story of Maria Korzelius, the intrepid hero in my ancestry. I'm also including parts of "The Healing Village," (Das Heilsame Dorf) because that's where my grandmother, another heroic woman in my life, nurtured me for more than five years.

The reader may notice a shift in the point of view in Book Two. This is a deliberate shift to the first person narrator because I was the little girl in the story.

Marianne Tong, November 2012

Ich besprach meine Geschichte mit meinem Onkel in Deutschland und versprach ihm ich würde sie in deutsch übersetzen und ihm eine Kopie schicken. Auch hatte ich schon eine Geschichte von Macken geschrieben, "Das Heilsame Dorf," die ich in meinen Memoiren, ***The Little Girl That Could*** herausgab. Ich übersetzte und schickte auch diese Geschichte an meinen Onkel und eine Schulfreundin.

In ***Maria Lives!*** gebe ich die englische so wie die deutsche Version der Geschichte von Maria Korzilius, die unerschrockene Heldin meiner Herkunft. Ich schliesse auch einige Details aus "Das Heilsame Dorf" ein, weil dort meine Grossmutter, auch eine heldenhafte Frau meines Lebens, mich fünf Jahre sorgfältig pflegte.

Ein Leser kann eine Veränderung in dem Perspektiv im Zweiten Buch merken. Dieser neue Gesichtspunkt ist absichtlich, weil ich selbst das kleine Mädchen war.

Marianne Tong, November 2012

Acknowledgments

A book does not write itself. A writer generally needs a push to get started with a new idea. I want to thank my cousin Karin Roth, nee Jung, for giving me such a push. She had done some genealogical research in Germany and thought I might be interested in our common ancestry. Once I had the book finished, she helped me to rework the chapter about our grandmother. Without Karin this book would never have materialized at all.

Once I had decided to write the book in German and English on opposing pages, I needed to have some reliable editing. My husband, as always, was called into action and read through the first draft. His questions and suggestions helped me to pull the manuscript together. Later, a fellow writer, Richard Bunning, generously helped me to find those annoying little errors that manage to elude a writer but distract a reader. From my daughter Vivienne, I got valuable advice about keeping my story "in the moment."

I was not quite confident that my German langluage met the standards, so I sent the manuscript to several friends and relatives in Germany. My cousin, Gabi Gilles, nee Küppers, and another cousin, Conni Bach assured me that my book was well-written. A few days later, I received another vote of confidence from Gerd Knechtges, the son of my precious Mackener school friend Martha.

A special thanks goes to Manni Messing, the son of my cousin Annemi Messing, nee Küppers. Manni painstakingly proofed the manuscript and gave me invaluable advice about German punctuation and sentence structure.

Anerkennung

Ein Buch schreibt sich nicht von selbst. Der Schriftsteller braucht einen Schubs, um eine neue Idee in ein Buch zu verwandeln. Ich möchte mich besonders bei meiner Kusine Karin Roth, geb. Jung, bedanken, weil sie mir solch einen Schubs gab. Sie hatte unsere gemeinsame Herkunft recherchiert, und dachte, daß ich mich für ihren Fund interessiere. Als das Buch fast fertig war, half sie mir die Geschichte unserer Grossmutter zu berichtigen. Ohne Karin wäre dieses Buch nie geschrieben worden.

Als ich mich entschied, das Buch auf deutsch und englisch auf gegenüberliegenden Seiten zu schreiben, brauchte ich zuverlässige Überprüfung. Mein Mann las den ersten Versuch auf englisch sorgfältig durch. Seine Fragen und Vorschläge halfen mir alles zusammenzuziehen. Später wurde das Manuscript auch von einem bekannten englischen Schriftsteller, Richard Bunning, gelesen. Er fand die kleinen ärgerlichen Fehler die man so leicht verpasst, die aber den Leser stören könnten. Von meiner Tochter Vivienne bekam ich besonders wichtige Ratschläge über die Zeitpunkte der Geschichte.

Ich war mir nicht ganz sicher ob meine deutsche Schrift standardgemäss lesbar war. Meine Kusine, Gabi Gilles, geb. Küppers, und mein Cousin, Conni Bach, versicherten mir, daß die einige kleinen Fehlern in Interpunktion und Satzstellung nicht stören. Dann erhielt ich die Mitteilung von Gerd Knechtges, der Sohn meiner Schulfreundin, daß er mein Buch gelesen und gut verstanden hatte.

Ein ganz besonderer Dank an Manni Messing, der Sohn meiner Kusine Annemi Messing, geb. Küppers, weil er sich sorgfältig

. The sheaves are piled high for drying. Die Garben stehn in Kasten zum Trocknen

die Mühe gab, die Fehler zu verbessern und einige Vorschläge zu
machen.

Book One

. In 1947 the house in Macken was photographed by the author's stepfather, John Miller. The stories in this book took place in this house. Dieses Haus wurde von John Miller, Mariannes Stiefvater in 1947 fotografiert. Es ist dasselbe Haus, wo diese Geschichten stattfanden.

Erstes Buch

2005 The same house won an architectural prize. Dasselbe Haus gewann wegen dem Fachwerk einem Ehrenpreis

1835

Peter and Maria Hammes

"You know Luz, I haven't been feeling really well since my baby died last year," a very pale Elisabeth explained to her friend Lucille in 1835. Lucille was the midwife in Macken, a cozy village in the Hunsrück Mountains in Germany.

"I noticed that you haven't done much baking lately," Luz answered. The two friends had come to the Backes (a public bake house with two fire chambers) along with three other villagers to decide their starting times for the next day's baking. As customary, each woman had whittled a distinctive design into a tiny piece of wood and placed it in the apron one of the women was holding high. "Come here, Tilli," called Luz to a small girl playing nearby. "You get to draw the lots." The order of the draw determined the order of the starting times of the following day's baking.

After the draw, Elisabeth and Luz chatted a few more minutes before they went home. The dough for the bread had to be prepared today. Elisabeth placed a great heap of flour in a clean wooden bread trough, Then she formed a small crater in the middle where she put the prepared sourdough. A bit of last week's dough had been drying in a cloth bag hung over the kitchen stove for the necessary heat. She had prepared the dried sourdough with water before putting it into the hollowed-out heap of flour and mixing it with some of the flour. A half hour later, she kneaded the rest of the flour into the sourdough that had begun to ferment.

1835

Peter und Maria Hammes

„Weißt du, Luz, seit ich mein Kindchen vor sechs Monaten verlor, hab' ich mich garnicht mehr wohl gefühlt," jammerte Elisabeth mit einem ganz blaßen Gesicht. Ihre Freundin Luzille war auch die Hebamme in Macken, ein gemütliches Dorf im Hunsrück.

„Ja, ich hab' schon gemerkt, daß du in der letzten Zeit nicht viel gebacken hast," bemerkte Luz. Die zwei Freundinnen mit noch drei anderen Bauersfrauen zogen gerade die Lose am Backes (das Volksbackhaus mit zwei riesengroßen Backöfen). Wie üblich, jede Frau hatte ein Holzstückchen nach ihrem eigenen Muster geschnitzt. Luz rief ein Kind in der Nähe, „Komm her, Tilli, du darfst die Lose ziehen. Dann bestimmen wir in welcher Ordnung die Frauen am nächsten Tag backen können."

Danach schwätzten Elisabeth und Luz noch ein paar Minuten, aber dann gingen sie nach Hause. Der Brotteig mußte noch heute vorbereitet werden. In einer sauberen hölzernen Backtruhe wurde ein Haufen Mehl geschaufelt. Dann wurde eine kleine Grube in der Mitte vom Haufen für den Sauerteig ausgehöhlt. Ein kleines Teil des getrocknetem Sauerteig von der vorigen Backwoche hing in einem Säckchen beim Küchenherd wegen der nötigen Wärme. Mit Wasser angefertigt, tat man denn den Sauerteig in die Grube und mischte diese Flüssigkeit mit etwas von dem Mehl. Eine halbe Stunde später knetete man den Rest von dem Mehl mit dem Sauerteig zusammen. Am Abend fing es schon im Haus gut zu riechen an.

17

The dough had to be kneaded again the next day before taking it to the Backes where it would be baked into bread.

The next day, Elisabeth dragged the dough and the wood to the Backes in a small wagon. Her six-year-old daughter, Liz, pushed the stroller in which little two-year-old Anton ruled the roost. This morning the air was still moist and cool, but in the Backes it would soon become warm and cozy. Once the fire was started, she placed the dough on the large wooden slab where she would knead it again and shape the loaves. She had enough dough for six large loaves of bread with a bit left over for the children's treat. The work was difficult for Elisabeth this morning. Every now and then she had to stop and gasp for air.

Finally the fire chamber was hot enough to bake the bread. Elisabeth grabbed the scraper on a long handle to sweep the ashes and the still-glowing cinders out of the oven. Then she used a clean wooden paddle to start pushing the loaves into the oven as far as they would go. She felt a moment of nausea and leaned against the wooden slab. Just then Luz arrived with her bread-making stuff. "Good morning, Elisabeth."

"Morning, Luz," Elisabeth gave a weak smile.

"And how are you, Little Liz?" Luz turned to the little girl near her mother. Her little brother with his rosy cheeks sat quietly in his stroller playing with an apple.

"I'm alright, Auntie Luz, but my mommy was crying again this morning," the child was not her usual bouncy self.

Dieser Teig wurde am nächsten Tag nochmal geknetet und dann im Backes zu Brot gebacken.

Am nächsten Tag schleppte Elisabeth den Teig und das Holz auf einem kleinen Leiterwagen in den Backes. Ihr sechs-jähriges Töchterchen, Liz, schob den Kinderwagen worin Anton, ihr zwei-jähriger Sohn herrschafte. Am frühen Morgen war die Luft noch feucht und kühl, aber im Backes würde es bald schön warm und gemütlich werden. Der Teig reichte für sechs große Laiber Brot. Erst nachdem sie das Holz im Ofen angezündet hatte, konnte sie den Teig nochmal auf dem grossen Holzbrett kneten und verteilen. Solche Arbeit fiel in der letzten Zeit Elisabeth sehr schwer. Sie hielt oft an, um ein bißchen Luft zu schnappen.

Endlich war Elisabeths Backofen heiß genug für das Brot. Elisabeth nahm eine Art Harke-Schaufel mit einem langen Stiel womit sie die Kohlen und Asche aus dem Ofen kehren konnte. Dann nahm sie den sauberen Schieber um die Teiglaiber in den Ofen zu schieben. Es wurde ihr schlecht, so lehnte sie sich an das Holzbrett. Luzille kam gerade mit ihrem Zeug in den Backes. „Guten Morgen, Elisabeth."

„Morgen, Luz," antwortete sie ganz schwach.

„Und wie geht's dir, Lizchen?" Luzille wendete sich zu dem kleinen Mädchen beim Kinderwagen worin der kleine Anton brav mit seinen roten Bäckchen saß. Er spielte mit einem Apfel.

„Mir geht's gut, Tante Luz, aber die Mami hat heute morgen wieder geweint," erwiderte das Kind.

"Come, Elisabeth, let me push the loaves into the oven. What is actually going on with you? You're not looking well at all. Why have you been crying?" Luz, a trained midwife, was very worried about the young woman.

"I believe I'm having another baby. I've hardly recovered from the stillbirth three months ago. It's too soon! Unless I'm mistaken, I'll have the baby in February. Anton is still in diapers! Little Liz is only six years old and can't help very much. What am I supposed to do?" Like marbles, the words came tumbling out of her mouth as she wiped her tear-streaked face with her flour-bespeckled apron.

For a moment everything was silent, but then the little girl said, "Mommy, aren't you going to make my applebread?" Luz and Elisabeth gave each other meaningful looks.

Elisabeth said, "Bring me that apple, Liz. I'll dice it and knead it into the rest of this dough. See, I even brought a bit of sugar, so that the applebread will taste especially good." She kept busy fixing the child's snack as Luz started to prepare her dough on the wooden slab.

"Elisabeth, you know that I'll help you as much as possible, but February is a hard month. It will probably be very cold. Is your house good and tight against the wind and rain?"

Gradually, Elisabeth began to feel a bit better. "Yes, my husband Peter is the only blacksmith in Macken. This year he did quite well. We have plenty of wood and our root cellar is filled.

„Komm Elisabeth, laß mich die Brote 'reinschieben. Was ist denn eigentlich los mit dir? Du siehst gar nicht gut aus. Warum hast du dann wieder geweint?" Luz machte sich Sorgen um die junge Frau.

„Ich glaube ich bekomme wieder ein Kind. Ich bin kaum von dem verstorbenen Kind geheilt! Es ist noch zu früh! Wenn ich mich nicht irre, kommt das Kind im Februar. Der Anton ist noch in Windeln! Lizchen ist erst sechs Jahre alt und kann noch nicht viel helfen. Was soll ich bloß?" Die Wörter kamen ihr nur so aus dem Mund gefallen als sie sich mit ihrer mehlbefleckten Schürze das Gesicht abwischte.

Einen Moment wurde es ganz still, aber dann meldete sich das Mädchen. „Mami, machst du denn nicht den Apfelplatz?" Luz und Elisabeth guckten sich bedeutend einander an.

Elisabeth sagte, „Bring mir den Apfel. Ich schneide ihn in kleine Würfel und knete sie dann in diesen Rest vom Teig. Siehst du, ich habe sogar ein bißchen Zucker mitgebracht, damit das Apfelbrot besonders gut schmeckt." Sie beschäftigte sich mit dem Apfelbrot als Luz ihren Teig auf der Holzplatte zu kneten anfing.

„Elisabeth, du weisst, daß ich dir so viel helfe wie möglich, aber Februar ist ein harter Monat. Es wird sehr kalt. Ist euer Haus auch gut dicht gegen den Wind und Regen?"

Es wurde Elisabeth ein wenig besser. „Ja Peter, mein Mann, ist ja der einzige Schmied in Macken. Dieses Jahr hat er's gut verdient. Wir haben auch genug Holz angelegt. Unser Keller ist voll

21

We have potatoes, turnips and lots of preserves including syrup. We also have a large crock of sauerkraut and a crock of pickled green beans. Then there are sacks of dried peas, lentils and beans. The dried apples are also stored in the cellar. We have plenty of flour and even a few bottles of beechnut oil. Our chickens are healthy and lay eggs daily and our three cows give milk. We also have sausages and bacon from the pig we slaughtered. We don't need to worry about our food supply, but my health is a different story. I feel so weak and tired, especially in my lower belly. I can't even imagine how I will manage with another baby."

Luz nodded with understanding, "When a woman has already buried a child…."

In his stroller, Anton started to whimper. He was only two years old and wanted to climb out. "Stay in your seat. Pretty soon you'll get a piece of the freshly baked applebread. Mmmm, that will be a yummy treat!" Elisabeth forced herself to pretend being in a good mood.

Luz had already started to heat up the second fire chamber. There was never enough time on "baking day" to discuss all kinds of personal problems. First the ladies had to think about the bread. Soon others would arrive with their baking supplies. Elisabeth waved as she was leaving. "Bye, Elisabeth, I'll come by this afternoon. Then we can talk over a good cup of coffee and fresh bread."

"Bye, Luz, till later!" Elisabeth pushed the stroller and little Liz was allowed to pull the cart filled with the aromatic fresh bread. On the way home, they heard the hammering in Peter's forge.

Kartoffeln, Rübenkraut, und eine Menge Eingemachtes. Wir haben auch einen Krug Sauerkraut und einen Krug Bohnensalat angelegt. Dann haben wir Säcke voll Erbsen, Linsen, Bohnen, und getrocknete Äpfel. Mehl und Bucheckernöl haben wir auch. Unsere Hühner legen Eier, und die drei Kühe geben Milch. Wir sind auch mit Würsten und Speck gut versorgt. Über unseren Vorrat brauch' ich mir dieses Jahr keine Sorgen zu machen. Aber mir ist es einfach nicht wohl im Unterleib, und ich bin immer so schwach und müde. Ich kann mir nicht vorstellen wie ich mit noch einem Kindchen zurechtkomme."

Luz nickte verständnisvoll, „Wenn eine Frau schon ein Kind beerdigt hat..."

Im Kinderwagen fing Anton zu wimmern an. Er war zwei Jahre alt und wollte aussteigen. „Bleib schön sitzen, bald bekommst du ein Stück von dem guten frischgebackenen Apfelbrot. Mmm, der wird wohl lecker sein!" Elisabeth zwang sich guter Laune zu täuschen.

Luz fing schon den zweiten Backofen aufzuheizen an. Es gab an einem Backmorgen nicht genug Zeit alle mögliche Probleme zu besprechen. Jetzt mußte man zunächst an das Brot denken. Bald würden die anderen Frauen mit ihrem Backzeug ankommen. „Tschüss, Elisabeth, ich komme heute Nachmittag bei dir vorbei. Dann machen wir uns eine gute Tasse Kaffee."

„Tschö, Luz, bis später!" Elisabeth schob den Kinderwagen, und Lizchen durfte den Leiterwagen mit den Broten heimziehen. Auf dem Heimweg konnte man schon das Hämmern in der Schmiede

Peter worked diligently when he was in his workshop or when he was working in his fields or with the animals, but Elisabeth could not depend on him to help in the house. For weeks she had been begging him to repair the outhouse next to the manure pile. It was impossible to sit on the broken boards without danger of falling in. Now the family had to depend on the hated chamber pot. "It's so disgusting!" she thought. "He'd better repair the outhouse before Winter."

"Mommy, Mommy! Anton won't let go of my braids." Liz was crying.

"No time to feel sorry for myself," thought Elisabeth as she ran to untangle the children. She gave both a tap on the backside before she handed them each a piece of the applebread. Then she placed large loaves into the wooden bread box. Now it was time to prepare the midday meal of fried potatoes with diced bacon, a dish of whey and applesauce. "Peter, time to eat!" Her voice, a little stronger now, could be heard in the smithy.

After the meal, Peter noticed Elisabeth's fearful face. A little too gruffly, he asked, "What's the matter, Elisabeth?"

"Peter, I am very fearful about this new baby. But I don't know why. Everything was going so well when we were first married. Now I simply don't feel good. It will be Christmas soon, but I'm not in the mood to think about Christmas presents. It's even difficult for me to decorate a little tree." Elisabeth had begun to whine as she quietly complained to her husband.

hören. Peter war fleißig, wenn es mit seiner Schmiede oder mit
Ackerbau und Viehzucht zu tun hatte, aber im Haushalt konnte
Elisabeth sich nicht auf ihn verlassen. Wochenlang bettelte sie wegen
dem Häuschen neben dem Misthaufen. Man konnte nicht mehr auf
dem Brett ohne Gefahr sitzen. Jetzt mußte sie das verhaßte Töpfchen
unter'm Bett gebrauchen. „So was ekelhaftes!" dachte sie. „er soll mir
ja den Klo vor dem Winter reparieren!"

„Mami, Mami! Anton läßt meinen Zopf nicht los!" Lizchen
war am Heulen.

„Keine Zeit um mir selbst Leid zu tun," dachte Elisabeth, als
sie zu den Kindern rannte. Sie gab beiden einen Klaps auf den Popo
ehe sie ihnen ein Stück von dem Apfelbrot reichte. Sie legte die
großen Brote in den Brotkasten, und dann wurde es Zeit das
Mittagessen vorzubereiten. Es gab Bratkartoffeln mit Speck,
Sauermilch und Apfelkompott. „Peter, komm essen!" rief sie in die
Schmiede.

Nach dem Essen sah Peter Elisabeths ängstliches Gesicht an.
Grob fragte er, „Was is los, Elisabeth?"

„Peter, ich habe richtig Angst um dieses neue Kind. Ich weiß
aber nicht warum. Wir hatten es so gut als wir jung verheiratet
waren. Jetzt fühle ich mich einfach nich mehr wohl. Bald ist es
Weihnachten, und ich habe gar keine Lust mich um Geschenke zu
kümmern. Mir fällt es sogar schwer ein Bäumchen zu schmücken."
Elisabeth jammerte leise zu ihrem Mann.

"Don't worry about a thing." Peter said, wanting to be helpful, but thinking of his own needs first. "What in the world am I going to do with two or three small children if Elisabeth dies in childbirth?" As a business-like blacksmith and simple husband, he couldn't feel any empathy with his whining wife. "Why don't you ask Lucille if has something to help you?" And with that, the matter was taken care of as far as he was concerned. "I still have a lot of work this afternoon and need to go back to the forge. Bye, Little Liz and Anton," he leaned briefly over the children and left the kitchen.

January was a mild month, but February brought a strong blizzard. Lucille forced her way through the thick snow to be at Elisabeth's side for the birth. Instinctively, she knew that she had to help with this birth because Elisabeth was not doing well at all. For three weeks she had already been bed-ridden. Kind neighbors had been bringing food and taking care of Peter and the children. Many prayed for Elisabeth, but hope was slim.

"In the name of the Father and the Son and the Holy Ghost, I baptize you Maria Margaretha," the priest sadly whispered the words over the tiny baby. In secret, he prayed a special prayer for the deceased mother. There would be no mother's milk for the weak child that was unable to tolerate any other nourishment. A week later the tiny angel was buried among the graves in the children's cemetery where the gravestones were decorated with white angel statues. Far too many children had already found their final resting place here. What kind of evil had bedeviled the village despite the plentiful harvests?

There was no answer.

„Mach dir doch keine Sorgen," Peter wollte behilflich sein, aber heimlich dachte er zunächst an seine eigene Not. „Was soll ich bloß mit zwei oder drei kleinen Kindern, falls Elisabeth im Kinderbett stirbt?" Als sachlicher Schmied und einfacher Ehemann konnte er kein Mitleid für seine jammernde Frau beibringen. „Frag doch mal Luzille ob sie irgendein Mittel hat, um dir zu helfen." Und damit war die Sache für ihn erledigt. „Ich hab noch viel Arbeit heute Nachmittag und muß jetzt in die Schmiede zurück. Tschüss, Lizchen und Anton," er lehnte sich kurz über die Kinder und verließ die Küche.

Januar war ein milder Monat, aber im Februar kam ein starker Schneesturm. Die Hebamme Luzille drang sich durch den dicken Schnee, um Elisabeth mit ihrer Niederkunft zu helfen. Sie wußte, daß sie unbedingt helfen mußte, denn Elisabeths Zustand sah nicht gut aus. Drei Wochen lag die kranke Mutter schon im Bett. Ihre Nachbarn hatten sich um Peter und die Kinder gekümmert. Man betete um Elisabeth, aber die Hoffnung war gering.

„Im Namen des Vaters, des Sohnes und des Heiligen Geistes, taufe ich dich Maria Margaretha," flüsterte traurig der Pfarrer über das kleine Kindchen während er heimlich ein Gebet für die verstorbene junge Mutter betete. Es gab keine Muttermilch für das arme Kind. Es war nicht kräftig und konnte keine andere Nahrung vertragen. Eine Woche später wurde das kleine Engelchen auf dem Kinderfriedhof zwischen den kleinen Gräbern mit den weißen Engelfiguren beerdigt. Viel zu viele Kinder lagen schon hier. Welches Unheil hatte dieses Dorf trotz der üppigen Ernte betroffen?

Es gab keine Antwort.

All winter long Peter was wrapped in deep grief and despair. His little Anton and dear little Liz needed a mother. Peter needed a wife! He couldn't continue to depend on his helpful neighbors forever. His tortured soul mirrored the miserable winter weather. But as the sun began to warm the air, and blossoms began to brighten the trees, he sensed a touch of hope. He needed to find a future for his family. On Easter Sunday, he took his children to church.

A group of young ladies had assembled on the plaza in front of the church. Peter, holding little Anton's hand, noticed an especially lively, attractive young woman in a pretty summer dress. He thought, "She must be from another village. I've never seen her before." Casually, Peter approached the cheerful group.

"Oh, how cute! How old is the little boy? What's his name?" Maria Korzilius called out to Peter. The other girls laughed at her.

"Careful, Maria, that man is a widower! He is probably looking for a new wife," whispered Magda, her blonde girlfriend. The other girls laughed.

"It's fine, I'm looking for a husband, so everything is in order!" whispered Maria to Magda. Then she turned back to Peter, "Please excuse me, I didn't mean to be so bold!"

Peter smiled, "His name is Anton, and one of these days he will become a talented blacksmith like myself." He tipped his hat briefly and walked away.

Peter weilte den ganzen kalten Winter in tiefer Trauer. Sein kleiner Anton und das liebe Lizchen brauchten eine Mutter. Peter brauchte eine Frau! Er konnte sich doch nicht auf die lange Dauer auf seine Nachbarn verlassen. Seine Seele spiegelte sich im schlechten Winterwetter, aber als die Sonne die Luft wärmte und die Bäume wieder blüten, schöpfte er Hoffnung. Am Ostersonntag ging er mit seinen Kindern zum Gottesdienst.

Eine Gruppe junger Frauen hatte sich auf dem Platz vor der Kirche versammelt. Peter mit seinem Antonchen an der Hand bemerkte ein besonders lebhaftes Fräulein in einem reizenden Sommerkleid. Peter spazierte gelassen in die Nähe der lachenden Gruppe. Er dachte, "Sie muß aus einem anderen Ort sein. Ich habe sie noch nie gesehn."

„Ach, wie goldig! Wie alt ist der Kleine? Wie heißt er?" Maria Korzilius rief Peter zu. Die anderen Mädchen machten sich lustig.

„Vorsicht, Maria, der Mann is Witwer! Er will sich bestimmt eine Frau anschaffen." flüsterte ihre blonde Freundin namens Magda.

„Also gut, ich suche einen Mann, so ist alles in Ordnung!" erwiderte Maria leise. Dann wandt sie sich zu Peter, „Verzeihung, ich wollte nicht so dreist sein!"

Peter lächelte, „Er heißt Anton, und eines Tages wird er ein begabter Schmied wie ich werden." Er tippte kurz seinen Hut und ging weiter.

Magda elbowed Maria in the side, "See? I knew it! Peter is absolutely in search of a wife!" All the young ladies giggled and then scurried in their billowing Sunday dresses toward the church. "Hurry up, everybody. Mass is about to start," called Magda at the front of the bunch.

Little Liz, who had been staring at Maria, ran after her father, "Daddy, who is that beautiful lady? Will she be my new mommy?"

"Whatever gave you that idea? What makes you think that I'm looking for a new mommy?" Peter joked with Little Liz.

"I would like to have a mommy, and that pretty lady seems very nice. You shouldn't be so sad all the time, Daddy." Liz had given words to her father's thoughts.

Peter made good use of this year's magnificent spring by wooing pretty Maria. Almost every evening he took the time to visit Maria and her parents in Burgen, the Mosel village. She was very friendly, and it was easy to see that she liked Peter. The wedding took place shortly after the harvest that year, and she moved into Peter's neglected house. Before the hard winter got underway, Peter had completely renovated the place. He repaired the outhouse and gave the well a new pulley, rope and bucket. He even ordered a new kitchen stove for his bride.

With her ambition and diligence Maria restored order in the home and motherly love to the children. With her robust good health at twenty-eight she already had the maturity of an experienced homemaker. All the work was easy for her. In the spring of 1837, she

Magda stieß Maria in die Rippen mit ihrem Ellbogen. „Siehst du! Ich hab's ja gewußt! Er ist ganz bestimmt auf der Suche nach einer Frau!" Alle Fräuleins kicherten und liefen in ihren bunten aufgebauschten Röcken zur Kirche. „Mach schnell! Die Messe fängt gleich an," rief Magda an der Spitze.

Lizchen kam hinter Peter her gerannt. „Vati, wer war die schöne Frau? Wird sie meine neue Mami?"

„Wie bist du auf diese Idee gekommen? Warum meinst du, daß ich eine neue Mami suche?" Peter scherzte mit Lizchen.

„Ich hätte gern eine Mami, und die schöne Frau war sympatisch. Du sollst nicht immer so traurig sein, Vati." Lizchen hatte Worte zu den Gedanken ihres Vaters gegeben.

Peter nutzte den prachtvollen Frühling aus. Fast jeden Abend fand er die Zeit um Maria und ihre Eltern im Moseldorf Burgen, zu besuchen. Sie war sehr freundlich und man konnte merken, daß Peter ihr gefiel. Die Hochzeit nahm kurz nach der Ernte statt, und sie zog in das vernachlässigte Haus Peters ein. Ehe der harte Winter einsetzte, wurde alles wieder renoviert. Peter reparierte das Abhäuschen und gab dem Brunnen eine neue Rolle, Seil und Eimer. Er kaufte sogar einen neuen Küchenherd für seine Braut.

Mit ihrem Fleiß und Eifer brachte Maria das Haus und die Kinder in Ordnung. Mit ihrer robusten Gesundheit und ihren achtundzwanzig Jahren hatte sie schon die Reife einer ausgebildeten Hausfrau. Alle Arbeit ging ihr leicht von der Hand. Im Frühjahr

became aware of the life growing within her. Little Balthasar was born in June. He was a strong little boy who would probably grow up to become a blacksmith like his father. The entire home sparkled with pride and joy.

Little Liz followed the example of her new mother and looked after her little brothers while Maria was busy with the preserving and storing of their winter food supply. Despite all the housework, Maria took time to serve a cup of coffee and a piece of cake whenever Luz visited her. Luz, the village midwife, had helped with the birth of Balthasar and also introduced Maria to the other village women who gathered regularly in front of the Backes or at church. Although she came from a rival village, Maria was readily accepted and soon became a real Mackener.

Depite an especially hard winter, little Philip was born healthy in February 1839. Peter took a deep breath as Luz told him that his third son was also a healthy strong child. His family was getting bigger and stronger. Only in an occasional quiet moment did Peter think about the mother of Liz and Anton, the beautiful but weak Elisabeth. His life had regained its balance, and everything appeared to be back in order. His growing daughter, Liz, kept a close eye on her healthy little brothers. His son, Anton would be attending school in the following year. What more could a man want?

Two years later little Johann arrived in the world. Peter was very proud. His daughter, Liz, and his four healthy sons, gave him

1837 spürte sie die Lebenszeichen eines Kindchens in ihr. Der kleine Balthasar wurde im Juni geboren. Er war ein kräftiger Junge, der wahrscheinlich auch ein Schmied wie sein Vater werden könnte. Das ganze Haus glänzte vor Stolz und Freude.

Lizchen ahmte dem Exemplar ihrer neuen Mami nach und versorgte die kleinen Buben während Maria mit dem Einmachen und Lagern des Lebensmittelvorrat beschäftigt war. Trotz der grossen Hausarbeit nahm Maria sich Zeit eine Tasse Kaffee aufzustellen, wenn immer Luzille sie besuchte. Luz hatte ihr mit der Geburt Balthasars beigestanden und stellte Maria auch den anderen Bauersfrauen, die sich beim Backes und in der Kirche versammelten, vor. Maria wurde freundlich empfangen, und bald wurde sie eine richtige Mackener Frau.

Trotz einem besonders harten Winter, wurde der kleine Philip im Februar 1839 geboren. Peter atmete tief auf, als Luzille ihm mitteilte, daß sein dritter Sohn auch ein gesunder Junge war. Seine Familie wurde immer grösser und stärker. Nur ab und zu in einer stillen Stunde dachte Peter an die Mutter von Liz und Anton, die schöne, aber schwache Elisabeth. Sein Leben hatte wieder sein Gleichgewicht gefunden, und alles schien in Ordnung zu sein. Die kleine Liz wollte ihre Brüderchen garnicht aus den Augen lassen. Anton war nahe an dem Alter wo er nächstes Jahr in die Schule gehen sollte.

Zwei Jahre später kam der kleine Johann auf die Welt. Peter war stolz. Seine Tochter Liz und seine vier gesunde Söhne gaben ihm

the hope that the sinister clouds which hovered above his first family had finally disappeared. He diligently worked in his forge and in the fields to provide a comfortable living for his family.

"Come here, Lizchen," called Maria one day after she had just cleared the breakfast dishes. "I need to measure you."

"Why? What are you doing with that measuring tape?"

"Do you still remember my girlfriend, Magda?"

"Yes, Mommy, I remember that you and the other girls ran away when my daddy was talking to you in front of the church," laughed Lizchen. "But why do you want to measure me?"

"Magda is getting married soon. She would like you to be her flower girl and carry her veil, so you'll need a new dress. Look at this beautiful material she bought in the city. I'm going to sew you a pretty dress for the wedding."

"Mommy, I didn't know that you can sew too," Lizchen was surprised. "Do you have a sewing machine?"

"Yes, I learned how to sew when I was still very young. After I was finished with school, I became an apprentice to a professional dressmaker. Before I got married, I even earned money with my trade, but I didn't bring my sewing machine to Macken. It's still at my parents' in Burgen. Tomorrow, your daddy is going to pick it up with the oxcart. You can ride with him to see your grandparents. I'll be able start on your new dress when I get the machine."

die Hoffnung, daß die dunkle Wolke, die über seiner ersten Familie hing jetzt endgültig verschwunden war. Eifrig arbeitete er in seiner Schmiede und auf den Feldern, um seine Familie zu versorgen.

„Komm her, Lizchen, ich much dich mal messen," rief Maria eines Tages kurz nachdem sie das Frühstücksgeschirr abgespült hatte.

„Warum, Mami? Was machst du mit dem Metermaß?"

„Kannst du dich noch an meine Freundin, Tante Magda erinnern?"

„Ja, Mami, ihr seid damals vor der Kirche weggelaufen," lachte Lizchen. „Aber warum willst du mich denn messen, Mami?"

„Magda wird bald heiraten und hat dich eingeladen den Schleier zu tragen. Dazu brauchst du ein neues Kleid. Guck mal, sie hat diesen schönen Stoff aus der Stadt mitgebracht. Ich nähe dir ein entzückendes Kleid für die Hochzeit," erklärte Maria.

„Mami, ich hab' ja garnicht gewusst, dass du auch nähen kannst," staunte Lizchen. „Hast du denn eine Nähmaschine?"

„Ja, ich habe das Nähen gelernt, als ich noch ein junges Mädchen war. Mit vierzehn kam ich aus der Schule und dann ging ich bei einer Schneiderin in die Lehre. Früher habe ich sogar mit meinem Nähen Geld verdient, aber meine Nähmaschine habe ich nicht nach Macken mitgebracht. Sie ist noch in Burgen. Dein Vati fährt morgen mit der Ochsenkarre nach Burgen um sie abzuholen. Du darfst mitfahren und deine Oma besuchen. Wenn die Maschine hier ist, fange ich mit dem neuen Kleid an."

"Mommy, may I watch?"

"Yes, we'll arrange a comfortable place for us and the boys in the parlor. Your dress will soon get done."

Lively, strong and always cheerful, Maria did not expect any difficulties in her everyday life. No bad news came to Macken from neighboring villages or cities; otherwise, she might have been able to protect herself against the evil that was about to befall her. It was not unusual for a less vigorous villager to succumb the way Peter's first wife had, but no one thought that such deaths had anything to do with the outside world. When little Philip first suffered from diarrhea in Juli 1842, Maria thought nothing of it. She simply cleaned things up and cared for him. Three days later she called Lucille.

"Luz, little Philip has soiled his pants three days in a row. He doesn't want to eat or drink. What could be wrong with him?" Maria was worried.

Lucille remained calm, "Maria, it's just a childhood illness. Philip is a robust little boy. Give him a few sips of tea every half hour till his appetite comes back." She didn't want to alarm Maria. That's why she didn't say anything about the other village youngsters that were also lying in their sickbeds.

"Mommy, I don't feel good!"

"What? You too, Balthasar?" Maria took a tired look at him. For the next few days both boys were sick. Maria was exhausted from the constant clean-up.

„Mami, darf ich dir zugucken?"

„Ja, wir machen uns hier in der Stube mit den Jungchen gemütlich. Dann wird das Kleid bald fertig."

Lebhaft, stark und immer heiter, Maria erwartete keine Schwierigkeiten in ihrem Alltagsleben. Man hörte auch keine schlimme Nachrichten aus der Umgebung Mackens oder aus den Städten; sonst hätte man sich vielleicht gegen das Übel schützen können. In dem Dorf starb manchmal ein Kindchen wie auch in Peters erster Familie, aber niemand dachte, daß ein solcher Tod irgendwas mit der Außenwelt zu tun hätte. Als der kleine Philip im Juli 1842 Durchfall bekam, regte sich Maria nicht auf. Sie machte einfach alles sauber und pflegte ihn. Drei Tage später rief sie Luzille.

„Luz, Philipchen hat schon drei Tage hintereinander seine Hose beschmutzt. Er will nichts essen oder trinken. Was könnte nur los mit ihm sein?" fragte Maria besorgt.

Luzille blieb ruhig, „Maria es ist bloß eine Kinderkrankheit. Philip ist ein kräftiger Junge. Gib ihm jede halbe Stunde paar Schlückchen Tee bis er wieder Appetit bekommt." Sie wollte Maria nicht Angst machen. Deshalb sagte sie nichts von den anderen Dorfkindern, die auch im Krankenbett lagen.

„Mami, mir ist's nicht wohl!"

„Was? Du auch Balthasar?" Maria schaute ihn müde an. Die nächsten paar Tage litten beide Jungen. Maria war erschöpft von dem ganzen Saubermachen.

"Help, help! My little Philip isn't breathing anymore," Maria screamed in a panic on a hot July day.

Holding baby Johann in her arms, Liz asked with a terrified face, "Mom, are we all going to die?" She got no answer except for a desperate shaking of the head.

Peter tried to remain brave, but he was pondering his fate. What had he done wrong? What was the matter with his family. Even his youngest son was beginning to show the symptoms of the same illness.

"No, no!" Maria screamed out the window into the sky. "All three babies dead!" Three or four times a week one could hear the blood-curdling screams of a mother in the village. Even the priest couldn't console the mothers. Every day the grieving mothers assembled on the cemetery, wondering, "What is happening to our children?" Their loud outcries were accompanied by Peter's frantic hammering in the forge. Sparks flew wildly into the air with each blow of the hammer on the hot anvil. Peter could not control himself. He didn't know that a new life was already growing in the body of Maria.

A tiny spark of hope arrived with a bountiful spring. Liz and Anton were healthy and thriving, and a new baby was on the way. A heavy burden, however, remained over Peter's family.

Maria forced her pregnant body with difficulty through the daily chores. The animals, the fields and the vegetable garden had

„Hilfe, Hilfe! Mein kleiner Philip atmet nicht mehr," in Panik versetzt, schrie Maria plötzlich in den heißen Julitag hinein.

Lizchen, mit dem kleinen Johann auf dem Arm fragte ängstlich, „Mami, sterben wir auch?" Sie bekam keine Antwort außer verzweifeltem Kopfschütteln.

Peter wollte tapfer bleiben, aber konnte nur über sein Schicksal grübeln. Was war mit seiner Familie los? Sogar sein jüngstes Söhnchen zeigte schon die ersten Symptome derselben Krankheit.

„Nein, nein!" Maria schrie aus dem Fenster, „Alle drei Kinderchen tot!" Durch's ganze Dorf hörte man drei-oder viermal in der Woche das grausame Geschrei der Mütter. Selbst der Pfarrer konnte sie nicht trösten. Jeden Tag versammelten sich trauernde Frauen, die Kinder verloren hatten, auf dem Friedhof. „Was ist bloß mit unseren Kindern passiert?" Ihr lautes Jammern wurde mit Peters hektischem Hämmern in der Schmiede begleitet. Funken flogen wie wild mit jedem Hammerschlag auf den heißen Amboß in die Luft. Peter konnte sich nicht fassen. Er wußte aber nicht, daß schon ein neues Leben in Marias Körper wuchs.

Mit dem Frühjahr kam eine kleine Hoffnung. Liz und Anton waren gesund aber eine schwere Last hatte sich über die Familie gelegt.

Maria zog mühsam ihren schwangeren Körper durch den Tag. Die Tiere, die Felder und der Gemüsegarten mußten gepflegt

to be taken care of. Bread had to be baked. There was no rest. Life went on, but Peter's house no longer glistened with pride.

Lorenz was born in the middle of April. Just like his deceased brothers, he was a vigorous little boy who could become a blacksmith one day. Maria and Peter didn't dare to think about the future. They simply held tight to each day with Liz, Anton and the new infant Lorenz.

One day, as Maria and Liz were occupied with the large harvest of peas, Maria looked at her daughter, "Liz, how would you like to have a little sister?"

"What do you mean? Are you having another baby?" Liz suddenly became cheerful.

"Yes, I'm having another baby in March, but I really don't know whether it will be a boy or a girl." Maria had been wondering how to approach the subject of human reproduction with little Liz. She had been waiting for an opportunity to talk about it, and now the moment was right. They were both sitting comfortably at the table, shelling peas for the winter food supply. Liz's capable young hands flew over the peas like little birds. In one swift move she opened the shell and tossed the peas into a bowl.

"Do babies grow like peas?" asked Liz.

und Brot gebacken werden. Ruhe gab es nicht. Das Leben ging weiter, aber Peters Haus glänzte nicht mehr.

In Mitte April kam Lorenz auf die Welt. Wie seine Brüder war er ein kräftiger Junge, der bestimmt auch Schmiede werden könnte. Maria und Peter konnten aber nicht an die Zukunft denken. Sie hielten sich Tag für Tag fest an Liz, Anton und den kleinen Lorenz.

Eines Tages, als Maria und Liz mit einer Ernte von Erbsen beschäftigt waren, fragte Maria, „Lizchen, wie wär's, wenn Du ein Schwesterchen bekämst?"

„Was meinst Du? Kriegst Du wieder ein Kindchen?" Liz heiterte im Moment auf.

„Ja, im März bekomme ich wieder ein Kind, aber ich weiß noch nicht, ob es ein Junge oder ein Mädchen ist." Maria hatte sich schon lange gewundert, wie sie das Thema der Natur mit Lizchen öffnen könnte und wartete auf eine Gelegenheit. Beide saßen gemütlich am Tisch und lasen die getrockneten Erbsen aus den Schalen für den Wintervorrat. Lizchens geschickte junge Hände flogen wie Vögel über die Erbsen. Mit einer Bewegung öffnete sie die Schale und warf die Erbsen in die Schüssel.

„Wachsen Kindchen wie Erbsen?" wollte Liz wissen.

"Not exactly like peas, Liz, but they do grow from very tiny in the body of a woman." Maria was glad that she now had the opportunity to explain the process. She continued, "Listen to me, Liz, I will explain to you how a baby gets into the body of a woman. You've watched a few times when Lambert's bull gave our cow a calf, haven't you? From that you can imagine how a man gives his wife a baby, can't you?"

"But Mom, you're not a cow!" indignant, Liz shouted out.

"You're right, Liz, but there are some similarities. Because we humans have souls, a man and his wife start out with love and respect for each other instead of simple animal desire. We can't forget that we are a species of animal, though. We are mammals. When a married couple is ready to start a family, the ability to…oh, you know!" Anton had just come through the door, so Maria got a bit embarrassed in front of the young boy. Liz winked with a knowing smile.

Liz called, "Come Anton, grab to, we need your help with these peas. We still have a lot of other work to do with the food supply for the winter."

Little Margaretha was born in March. The winter rains had already stopped, and the spring was promising to be mild. With small but healthy Lorenz and two strong helpful older children, Maria recovered quickly after the birth. Peter watched in satisfaction as Margaretha took easily to the breast of his wife. His heart also began to heal. He was certain, that after the death of his first wife and five

„Nicht genau wie Erbsen, aber sie wachsen von ganz, ganz klein in dem Körper einer Frau." Maria freute sich, daß sie jetzt die Gelegenheit hatte, den Prozess zu erklären. Maria fuhr fort, „Hör mir mal zu, Lizchen, und ich werde dir erzählen, wie so ein Kindchen in den Körper einer Frau kommt. Du hast doch mal zugeschaut wie Lamberts Bulle unserer Kuh ein Kalb gab. Davon kannst du dir auch vorstellen, wie ein Mann einer Frau ein Kindchen gibt, nicht wahr?"

„Aber du bist doch keine Kuh, Mami!" stoß Liz empört aus.

„Du hast Recht, Liz, aber da ist doch etwas gleich. Weil wir Menschen Seelen haben, fangen ein Mann und eine Frau mit Liebe und Respect an, anstatt mit tierischer Lust. Man soll aber nicht vergessen, daß wir doch eine Art Tier sind. Wenn ein Ehepaar eine Familie zu gründen bereit ist, dann haben wir die Fähigkeit...ach, Du weißt doch!" Anton kam gerade durch die Tür, und Maria genierte sich ein bißchen vor dem Junge. Liz blinzelte ihr mit einem wissenden Lächeln zu.

Liz rief, „Komm Anton, greif ein, wir brauchen deine Hilfe mit den Erbsen. Wir haben noch viel Arbeit bis der Wintervorrat fertig ist."

Die kleine Margaretha wurde im März geboren. Der Winterregen hatte schon aufgehört und der Frühling war mild. Mit dem kleinen kräftigen Lorenz, und zwei brave, behilfliche große Kinder, erholte sich Maria kurz nach der Geburt. Peter sah zufrieden zu als Margaretha an der Brust seiner Frau sog. Sein Herz fing auch wieder zu heilen an. Er war sicher, daß nach dem Tod seiner ersten

of his children, nothing could destroy his peace of mind. His family was bound to thrive this time.

"Maria, this year we have to be very frugal in handling our food supply. It's time to plant, but we need rain. It's been too dry. Without enough rain, our harvest will be very sparse."

"Peter, I guess we'll have to eat less and be careful not to waste our food," joked Maria. Despite her ominous premonitions, Maria kept her cheerful attitude. "We also need to pray twice as much as usual," she added with a laugh.

Just as Peter feared, there was no rich harvest in the summer of 1846. The year before, the rye and wheat harvest had promised abundant bread for the entire year, but this year there would be much less baking. Also the lack of clover and hay threatened the animals, and in turn the meat, milk and butter supply. There was not even the usual surplus of potatoes. No one could expect help from the neighboring villages because the harvest had been the same all over. With efficient rationing, the family would survive until the next harvest. The entire family had to be more frugal.

"Anton, go get me a bucket of water from the well. Little Margaretha just vomited, and I have to clean this mess up," Maria's heart was beating in fear. This is exactly how it started with Philip four years ago. Maria guarded her worried eyes in front of Anton and Liz. "Don't worry, maybe the soup I gave her for lunch didn't agree with her."

Frau und fünf seiner Kinder, es könnte ihn nichts mehr niederschlagen. Seine Familie wird jetzt gedeihen.

„Maria, dieses Jahr müssen wir sparsam mit unserem Vorrat umgehen. Es ist Zeit zum Pflanzen, aber wir brauchen dringend Regen. Ohne Regen wird die Ernte bestimmt mager sein."

„Peter, dann müssen wir eben weniger essen und vorsichtig mit unseren Lebensmittel umgehn," meinte Maria. Trotz ihrer unheimlichen Ahnung, setzte sie immer ein heiteres Gesicht auf. „Wir sollen zweimal so viel beten wie sonst," lachte sie noch dazu.

Wie Peter befürchtete, gab es im Sommer 1846 keine reiche Ernte. Im letzten Jahr versprach die Getreideernte genügend Brot für den ganzen Winter, aber dieses Jahr würde man weniger backen können. Auch der Mangel an Klee und Heu bedrohte das Vieh. Sogar der übliche gute Kartoffelüberfluß fand dieses Jahr nicht statt. Man konnte auch keine Hilfe von den Nachbardörfern erwarten, weil das Wetter überall dasselbe war. Mit schlauer Einteilung konnte man es doch durch einen Winter aushalten. Man müßte sich nur sehr gut beherrschen.

„Anton, geh hol' mir einen Eimer Wasser vom Brunnen. Die kleine Margaretha hat sich übergeben, und ich muß sie abwaschen," Marias Herz klopfte vor lauter Angst. So hatte es auch vor vier Jahren mit Philip angefangen. Maria schützte ihre Augen vor Anton und Liz. „Keine Angst, Lizchen, wahrscheinlich konnte Margretchen die Suppe, die ich ihr heute Mittag gab, nicht vertragen."

"Mommy, then what's wrong with Lorenz? He didn't eat any of the soup, but he just pooped on the floor. It's very stinky and liquidy," Liz asked.

"Liquidy? Did you mean that he had diarrhea?" Now Maria stopped trying to hide her fear. She screamed, "Come on, hurry up with that water! We need to clean everything thoroughly!"

"But, Mom, our well is almost dry! We don't have enough for the animals and for our household. How can we use the water to wash everything?" Liz started to cry just as Peter burst into the kitchen with an angry face.

"What's going on with you women? Anton complained to me that he was supposed to get water, but he couldn't lower the bucket deep enough to reach the water level. What do you need that much water for, anyway?' The muscles in his cheeks were showing his anger.

"Peter, Lorenz had diarrhea and Margaretha has vomited all over herself. I'm very scared for these babies. This is how it started last time. Why are we being punished like this? Why don't we even have enough water to keep the house clean?" Maria started to cry. "I can't take it anymore! I can't take it! I can't!" Maria stormed at Peter.

At that moment, little Margaretha vomited again. Peter felt an icy shudder pass across his spine. The terror of four years ago had returned to his home.

„Mami, denn was ist mit Lorenz los? Er hat doch keine Suppe gegessen und machte gerade auf den Boden. Es stinkt und ist flüssig," Liz war ganz verzweifelt.

„Flüssig? Meinst du, er hat Durchfall gehabt?" Jetzt hörte Maria ihre Angst zu verheimlichen auf. Sie schrie, „Komm, hol' Wasser! Wir müssen alles saubermachen!"

„Aber Mami, der Brunnen ist doch fast trocken! Wir haben nicht genug Wasser für die Tiere oder zum Kochen. Wie können wir denn alles abwaschen?" Liz fing zu heulen an, als Peter mit einem bösen Gesicht in die Küche kam.

„Was ist denn jetzt mit Euch Weibern los? Anton hat sich bei mir beschwert, daß er Wasser holen sollte, aber er konnte den Eimer nicht tief genug, um das Wasser zu erreichen senken. Warum braucht ihr denn so viel Wasser." Die Muskeln in seinen Backen wirkten ununterbrochen.

„Peter, Lorenz hat Durchfall und Margaretha hat sich bekotzt. Ich habe Angst um die zwei Kleinen. So fing es damals an. Warum werden wir denn so bestraft? Warum haben wir denn nicht mal genug Wasser um das Haus sauber zu behalten?" Maria fing an zu weinen. „Ich kann nicht mehr! Ich kann nicht mehr!" stürmte sie auf Peter zu.

In dem Moment übergab sich die kleine Margaretha wieder. Ein kalter Schauder lief über Peters Rückengrad. Der Schrecken des Übels war in sein Haus zurückgekehrt.

"Again two more dead babies! God! How can a family endure such suffering?" Peter roared at heaven through the open window.

For Peter the answer lay in his manhood! Only eleven months later Catherine was born. Her strong voice announced a fertile spring season and warm summer. Hints of a good year were appearing everywhere. The animals began to fatten up and the fields were turning green. Everyone in the village was expecting an abundant harvest.

"My goodness, Mother! What a lot of work this cabbage will take!" Liz was in the yard watching Peter and Anton unload a whole cart of cabbages.

Maria agreed. "Yes, but we shouldn't complain; instead, we should think about the near-starvation of last year. This year we'll have plenty of sauerkraut and all kinds of other stuff. We might even be able to send the surplus to the farmers' market in the city. Come, let's get started right away." Maria had already picked two buckets of raspberries. Today she had planned to preserve the raspberry concentrate for juice.

"Mother, what are we going to do with this mountain of apples? Anton picked them yesterday and put them in this bin," Liz was usually cheerful, but at the moment she seemed a bit annoyed, "and now we're supposed to do the work of peeling them."

Maria calmed Liz, "Little Liz, we're not going to work ourselves to death. While we're peeling the apples, we'll sing a few songs to make the work go faster. On Sunday we won't do any work.

„Wieder zwei tote Kinder! Wie kann eine Familie so ein Leid ausstehen?" brüllte Peter dem Himmel zu.

Für ihn lag die Antwort in der Natur! Bloß elf Monate später kam Catharina auf die Welt. Ihre starke Stimme kündigte einen fruchtbaren Frühling und Sommer an. Man konnte überall Erscheinungen eines guten Jahres erkennen. Die Tiere wurden wieder fett und die Felder grün. Im ganzen Dorf erwartete man eine üppige Ernte.

„Meine Güte, Mutter! Was haben wir Arbeit mit dem vielen Kappes!" Liz stand im Hof und schaute zu wie Peter und Anton einen Wagen Kohl entluden.

Maria meinte, „Ja, wir sollen uns aber nicht beschweren, sondern uns nur an die Hungernot vom letzten Jahr erinnern. Dieses Jahr gibt es genug Sauerkraut und alles Mögliche. Wir können sogar den Überfluss davon auf den Bauernmarkt in der Stadt schicken. Komm, wir fangen direkt an." Maria hatte schon zwei Eimer Himbeeren am frühen Morgen gepflückt. Sie wollte heute noch den Saft einmachen.

„Mutter, was machen wir denn mit diesem Berg Äpfel? Gestern hat Anton sie gepflückt und hier in die Truhe gebracht. Aber die Arbeit alle zu schälen sollen wir tun." Liz war sonst heiter und lustig, aber im Moment wurde sie doch ein bißchen ärgerlich.

Maria befriedigte Liz, „Lizchen, wir arbeiten uns nicht kaputt. Beim Schälen singen wir paar Lieder, und dann geht es wohl schnell voran. Am Sonntag arbeiten wir überhaupt nicht. Dann laden

Then we'll invite Aunt Luz and enjoy a nice afternoon with a good cup of coffee and a piece of coffee cake with your favorite crumbs." Liz was astonished at her dear stepmother.

"May I help with the raspberry juice?" Liz had regained her good mood. "Then you can explain what we're going to do with the peeled apples."

"Let's go to the kitchen, Liz. Tomorrow we'll start with the apples. First they need to be cleaned and sorted. The ones with worms or the ones that are starting to rot will get tossed into a big barrel. We're going to give them to our neighbor who distills schnaps out of rotten fruit. The best apples will be stored whole in our cool root cellar where they will last a long time. We call them table fruit because they can be eaten as they are. Then we'll take care of the ordinary middle sort. We'll peel them and cut them into small wedges. Then we'll take long pieces of this twine and a needle to string the wedges like a garland. I already have hooks near the ceilings in our bedrooms. We'll hang the apple garlands just under the ceiling where they will dry in the heat. It might take two weeks or so. Then we'll put the dried apple wedges into a wooden crate and store them in the cellar."

Liz was quite enthused now. "Mom, I just remembered that we stored some apples this way last year. Sometimes you made applesauce with them. I especially liked to eat the dried wedges like a snack. But why do we have so many more apples this year?"

wir Tante Luz ein, und ruhen uns mit einer guten Tasse Kaffee und einem Stück Streußelkuchen aus." Liz konnte nur über ihre liebe Stiefmutter staunen.

„Darf ich mit dem Himbeersaft helfen?" Lizchen war wieder guter Laune. „Dabei kannst du mir erzählen was wir mit den Äpfel machen."

„Komm in die Küche, Lizchen. Morgen fangen wir mit den Äpfel an. Zuerst werden sie sauber gemacht und sortiert. Die halbfaulen oder die mit Würmern werden in eine große Tonne geschmissen. Die geben wir gewöhnlich dem Nachbarn. Der macht Schnaps mit der faulen Frucht. Die besten Äpfel behalten wir frisch im Keller, wo sie sich in der Kühle länger halten. Die nennen wir Tafeläpfel, weil man sie so aus der Hand essen kann. Dann kommen die mittleren an die Reihe. Die werden geschält und in kleine Scheiben geschnitten. Dann nehmen wir eine lange Schnur und reihen die Apfelscheibchen auf. Im Schlafzimmer habe ich schon Haken ganz oben an der Decke. Daran lassen wir die Schnur hängen bis die Scheibchen ganz trocken sind. Vielleicht zwei Wochen. Dann kommen sie in eine Holzkiste im Keller." Maria hatte alles so schön erklärt, daß Lizchen ganz begeistert war.

„Mutter, jetzt kann ich mich erinnern, wie wir auch letztes Jahr die Äpfel so verwahrt haben. Dann hast du Apfelkompott damit gemacht. Ich habe auch gern so trockene Scheibchen gegessen. Aber warum haben wir dieses Jahr so viel mehr Äpfel?"

"Last year we didn't get enough rain. In such dry weather, the plants don't grow very well. All the food became scarce, and we had to be so frugal that we couldn't even bake a delicious coffeecake every week." Despite the ache in her heart as she thought about the horrible previous year, she remained hopeful. " I believe that this year we will have plenty of rye and wheat."

"Mother, what are we doing with the rye?" Little Liz only had a weak memory of her trip to the mill in Dommershausen.

"Liz, surely you can remember when your father took you along to Dommershausen. The miller there works the mill for all the surrounding villages. When a farmer brings his sacks of grain to the mill, the miller can use his machines to grind the grain into flour. The miller keeps part of the flour as his reward instead of money. Later he can do business with the flour he kept. Not all people can bake their own bread. In the cities, people buy their baked bread in bakeries. When you get a little older, we'll take a trip to a city, perhaps Koblenz or Trier. Then I will show you things that aren't even known here in the village," Maria loved to explain things to her attentive stepdaughter Liz.

Liz was very happy with her stepmother. Now she even had a healthy little sister named Catherine. Her brother Anton spent a lot of time in the forge with his father after the field work was done and the animals were taken care of. Liz was glad that he had finally stopped the constant teasing and bullying. As a result, Liz was able to spend a lot of time with Maria in the preparation of the food supply.

„Letztes Jahr hat es nicht genug geregnet. In so einem trockenen Wetter wachsen die Pflanzen nicht so gut. Alles war sehr knapp, und wir konnten noch nicht mal einen guten Streußelkuchen jede Woche backen," lachte Maria trotz dem Schmerz im Herzen, als sie an das vorige unfruchtbare, verheerende Jahr dachte. „Dieses Jahr haben wir auch viel Korn und Weizen."

„Mutter, was tut man denn mit dem Korn?" Lizchen hatte nur noch eine schwache Erinnerung an die Dommershauser Mühle.

„Liz, du kannst dich doch bestimmt erinnern, wie dein Vater dich nach Dommershausen mitgeholt hat. Der Müller dort führt die Mühle für alle Nachbarsdörfer. Wenn ein Bauer seine Säcke Getreide zu ihm bringt, kann der Müller es mit seiner Maschine zu Mehl mahlen. Der Müller behält dann ein Teil von dem Mehl als Lohn. Er kann dann später mit dem Mehl Geschäfte machen. Nicht alle Leute backen ihr eigenes Brot. In einer Stadt kaufen sie Brot von den Bäckereien. Wenn du mal groß genug bist, fahren wir mal in eine Stadt, vielleicht nach Koblenz oder Trier. Dann zeig ich dir Sachen die man garnicht hier im Dorf kennt." Maria erzählte der aufmerksamen Liz immer gern.

Liz war mit ihrer Stiefmutter sehr glücklich. Jetzt hatte sie auch ein gesundes Schwesterchen namens Catharina. Ihr Bruder Anton verbrachte viel Zeit mit seinem Vater in der Schmiede, nachdem die Feldarbeit fertig und das Vieh versorgt war. Er hat auch endlich mit dem Necken und Quälen, woran er immer viel Spaß hatte, aufgehört. Jetzt konnte Liz viel Zeit mit Maria, besonders mit

She especially enjoyed helping with the green beans. Maria had a little machine where one could guide a string bean into a top opening while cranking the handle. The bean came out in neat little French-cut slices that could be processed into pickled bean salad. Liz and Maria spend the entire summer working with the food preservation. Even little Catherine was thriving. On one such pleasant afternoon Liz suddenly asked Maria, "Mother, are we going to get any more babies?"

This took Maria by surprise, "At the moment I'm not expecting. Perhaps I won't get any more. It does not depend only on me. Sometimes a married couple doesn't get any children even though they would love to have some. That is the mystery of nature. Perhaps in the future, science will learn how to solve such problems, but nowadays we have no control over such things."

"Maybe my father is afraid to have any more children. He might think that all his sons will die, and so he doesn't want to give you any," thought Liz out loud.

"Liz, you might be right, but we have Anton who is your father's son. Your father is a good man. He works hard in the fields and in his forge. He's not afraid of anything. It is not his fault, that his babies died. And it's not his fault that I'm not expecting another child. It is simply nature. You will understand this once you get married." As Maria was talking, she noticed that Liz was blushing. "Liz, tell me, do you have a boyfriend? Do you think once in a while about getting married?"

der Vorbereitung von Lebensmittel, verbringen. Sie half besonders gern mit den grünen Bohnen. Maria hatte ein Maschinchen wo man oben eine Bohne reinsteckt, dann dreht man einen Henkel und unten kommen dann kleine Scheibchen, die man zum Bohnensalat einmacht `raus. Den ganzen Sommer verbrachten Liz und Maria die Zeit zusammen, und die kleine Catharina wuchs auch glücklich heran. An so einem gemütlichen Nachmittag fragte Liz, „Mutter werden wir noch mehr Kindchen bekommen?"

Maria war erstaunt, „Im Moment bin ich nicht in Hoffnung. Vielleicht bekomme ich keine mehr. Es ist ja nicht nur meine Sache. Manchmal bekommt ein Ehepaar überhaupt keine Kinder, obwohl sie gerne Kinder hätten. Das ist ein Geheimnis der Natur. Vielleicht lernt die Wissenschaft in der Zukunft wie man solche Probleme löst, aber heutzutage hat man keine Kontrolle über solche Dinge."

„Vielleicht will mein Vater aus Angst gar keine neue Kinder. Er meint vielleicht, daß ihm seine Söhne wegsterben. Und so will er dir keine mehr geben," meinte Liz.

„Liz, du könntest Recht haben, aber wir haben Anton, der ein Sohn deines Vaters ist. Dein Vater ist ein guter Mann. Er arbeitet schwer auf dem Feld und in seiner Schmiede. Er hat vor nichts Angst. Es ist nicht seine Schuld, daß die Kinderchen starben. Auch nicht, daß ich im Moment keins trage. Es ist einfach Natur. Das wirst du auch lernen wenn du mal verheiratet bist." Als Maria sprach, merkte sie, daß Liz rot angelaufen war. „Liz, hast du eigentlich einen Freund? Denkst du ab und zu ans Heiraten?"

Liz blushed. "Wel-l-l, there is Gerhard. You know who he is. On Sunday after Mass, he tried to kiss me, but I ran away."

"Liz, he is a dear boy, but don't be in a hurry." Then Maria thought, "This evening I'll have to talk to Peter about Liz. His daughter is almost at marriagable age."

"Luz, guess what!" Maria started the conversation over coffee. "I'm having another baby!" Lucille was a welcome visitor this Sunday afternoon.

Luz took a long look at Maria. "I think you are the bravest woman I know." Lucille was thinking about the other women in the village that had also lost babies in the 1842 and 1846 epidemics. Some of the women still hadn't recovered from the shock. They grieved their lives away, but Maria wasn't like that. After a reasonable period of mourning her losses, she started to live again. Most of the time, Maria appeared to be healthy and cheerful. One short year after the horrible deaths, she gave birth to a baby in 1847 and now she was happily announcing another pregnancy. "I can't imagine how you can be happy to have another baby. When is this baby due?" asked Luz.

"In April. By that time the weather should be nice and warm. There might be rain, but that shouldn't be a problem. Peter has taken good care of this house. We have a new roof, and all the windows and doors have been tightened against the cold air. He even built us

„Na ja, da ist Gerhard. Du kennst ihn. Am Sonntag nach der Messe hat er versucht mich zu küssen. Ich bin aber weggelaufen," gab Liz zu.

Maria lachte, „Er ist ein lieber Kerl, aber hab' keine Eile." Dann dachte sie heimlich, „Heute Abend bespreche diese Sache mal mit Peter. Seine Tochter ist fast im Heiratsalter."

„Luzille, was meinst du?" fing Maria beim Kaffeetrinken an. „Ich bekomme wieder ein Kind!" Luzille hatte Maria an diesem Sonntagnachmittag besucht.

Luz guckte Maria lang an. „Ich meine, du wärst die tapferste Frau die ich kenne." Luzille dachte an die anderen Frauen die auch Kinder in 1842 und 1846 verloren hatten. Manche davon hatten sich drei Jahre später immer noch nicht von dem Schreck erholt. Sie trauerten ihre ganze Lebenszeit weg, aber Maria machte es anders. Nach einem heilsamen Abstand von dem Schreck, fing sie wieder zu leben an. Maria wirkte meistens gesund und munter. Sie hatte auch schon 1847 ein Kindchen bekommen, und jetzt freute sie sich wieder. „Ich kann mir einfach nicht vorstellen warum Du froh bist, wieder ein Kind zu bekommen. Wann soll denn das Kind ankommen?" fragte Luz.

„Im April. Bis dahin soll das Wetter schon bißchen wärmer sein. Es gibt wahrscheinlich Regen, aber das ist ja nicht so schlimm. Peter hat das Haus in Schuß gebracht. Wir haben sogar ein neues Dach, und alle Fenster und Türen sind dicht. Er hat uns auch ein

a new outhouse after I told him about epidemics that might be transmitted through dirt and germs. He still isn't completely convinced that illness might be contagious. He still believes that he is being punished for some unknown sin he might have committed." Maria was in a happy mood. "You know, Luz, I always feel that I'm destined to become the mother of a large family. Who knows what will all be discovered by science? Perhaps in the future all these terrible epidemics will be controlled and all illnesses will be curable. I've heard some city people who travel through here talk about things like that."

Luz said, "You're dreaming, Maria! You shouldn't believe everything that these city travelers say. They don't know it all."

Maria laughed, "Yes, I know that. But at least Peter listens to me when I tell him about the city travelers. My parlor, that we hardly use, has become a small weekend pub. We've been making quite a bit of money from the city folk who travel through Macken."

Lucille took another piece of coffeecake. Maria poured her another cup of coffee. The two women carried on their conversation about the pub for a while longer. "I heard that even the Mackener villagers enjoy drinking a beer or two at the 'Hospese' after a hard day at work."

"Yes, Luz, some of them even order a bowl of soup or a platter of cold cuts. Liz helps in the kitchen, and Anton serves the food. Our little Catherine runs around to entertain the guests.

neues Häuschen gebaut nachdem ich ihm von den Krankheiten, die man durch Dreck kriegen kann erzählte. Er ist aber nocht nicht ganz überzeugt, daß es ansteckende Krankheiten gibt. Er meint immer noch, daß er durch irgendeine Sünde verdammt sei." Maria war guter Laune. „Weißt du, Luz, ich meine immer, daß ich als Mutter einer großen Familie bestimmt wäre. Wer weiß, was noch alles in der Wissenschaft erfunden wird und wie weit es die Menschheit noch bringt? In der Zukunft könnte man vielleicht alle diese schwere Seuchen beseitigen und alle Krankheiten heilen. Das habe ich von den Städterleuten gehört, die ab und zu bei uns halten."

Luz meinte, „Du schwärmst, Maria! Du darfst nicht alles, was die Städter sagen glauben. Die wissen auch nicht alles."

Maria lachte, „Ja, das weiß ich. Aber wenigstens hört Peter mir zu, wenn ich ihm etwas von den Städtern erzähle. Meine gute Stube ist am Wochenende wie eine kleine Wirtschaft geworden. Wir machen ganz gut Geld mit den Leuten, die durch Macken kommen."

Luzille nahm noch ein Stück Streußelkuchen. Maria schenkte ihr Kaffee ein. Die beiden Frauen unterhielten sich noch eine Weile über die Wirtschaft, die Maria gegründet hatte. „Ich hab gehört, daß selbst die Mackener gern am Abend bei „Hospese" ein Bierchen trinken gehn."

„Ja, Luz, manche bestellen sich sogar eine Suppe oder eine Kalte Platte. Liz hilft in der Küche und Anton bedient die Leute. Unser kleines Catharienchen läuft herum und unterhält die Gäste.

Peter is especially happy about the corner table that is always reserved for the regulars. There he can debate all kinds of subjects with his buddies." Maria became more and more animated as she described her rapidly growing pub. "We never really used our parlor before. Now we are making good use of the room."

Luz said good-bye after she was finished with her coffee and cake. "It was wonderful to be able to talk about such good news with you. Thanks for the food and good company," she added before she left.

Maria waved good-bye and thought, "I hope this baby will be a boy. I want Peter to get a son from me."

Peter ist besonders froh über den Stammtisch der sich mittlerweile entwickelt hat. Da kann er alle möglicheThemen mit seinen Kumpeln debattieren." Maria wurde ganz belebt, als sie ihre Wirtschaft beschrieb. „Wir haben die gute Stube sonst nie bewohnt. Jetzt machen wir guten Gebrauch von dem Raum."

Luz verabschiedete sich, nachdem sie mit dem Kuchen und Kaffee fertig waren. „Es war wunderbar etwas Erfreuliches mit dir zu besprechen. Vielen Dank für Speis und Trank," sagte sie noch ehe sie ging.

Maria winkte ihr nach und dachte, „Hoffentlich wird dieses Kindchen ein Junge. Peter soll einen Sohn von mir bekommen."

1866

Moritz Hammes

"Mother, where should I put these new beer steins?" called Moritz, who had become an energetic young man of sixteen. He was carrying a wooden crate of steins on his shoulder. It was a cool November, and the "Hospese Tavern" would most certainly become a cozy place for the locals to gather on those long evenings in the winter months.

Maria's voice rang from the kitchen, "The shelves behind the bar! But make sure that you wash all the steins first and wipe down the shelves." Maria valued cleanliness. It was certain now that many illnesses could be avoided by maintaining sanitary conditions. Sadly, it hadn't been possible to avoid Peter's death. "I wish your father could see how well his family is doing now." Moritz was only seven and his little sister Maria Anna only four when Peter had his accident in his blacksmith shop. He was kicked by the horse he was trying to shoe. Anton was present and called for help right away, but neither Lucille nor the new village doctor were able to bring Peter back to consciousness.

The reputation of "Hospese Tavern" kept increasing even after Peter's death. The local villagers met there at every chance. Maria's delicious meals attracted the most discriminating tastes. Catherine, the beautiful blond nineteen-year-old, waited on tables and played some songs on the new harmonium. Sixteen-year-old Moritz took

1866

Moritz Hammes

„Mutter, wohin soll ich die neuen Krüge stellen?" rief Moritz, der jetzt ein kräftiger Junge von sechszehn Jahre war. Auf seiner Schulter trug er eine Holzkiste mit Bierkrügen. Es war November, und die „Hospese Wirtschaft" würde bestimmt wieder eine gemütliche Gaststätte an den langen Winterabenden werden.

Marias Stimme schallte aus der Küche, „Die Regale hinter der Schenke! Aber mach ja, daß du die Krüge erst gut spülst und die Regale abwischst!" Maria legte viel Wert auf die Sauberkeit. Es hat sich festgestellt, daß man viele Krankheiten durch Sauberkeit vermeiden kann. Leider konnte sie nicht den Tod Peters vermeiden. „Ich wünsche dein Vater könnte mal sehn wie gut es seiner Familie geht." Moritz war nur sieben Jahre alt, und sein Schwesterchen Maria Anna gerade vier wie Peter den Unfall hatte. In der Schmiede tretete ihn ein Pferd an den Kopf als er das Hufeisen beschlagen wollte. Anton war dabei und rief direkt um Hilfe, aber Luzille und der neue Dorfarzt konnten Peter nicht mehr zu Bewußtsein bringen.

Der Ruhm der Hospese Wirtschaft nahm aber auch nach dem Tode zu. Die Dorfleute versammelten sich zu allen Gelegenheiten. Marias Gerichte lockten die verwöhntesten Gäste. Die schöne blonde Catharina, jetzt neunzehn, bediente die Gesellschaft, und manchmal spielte sie paar Lieder auf dem Harmonium welches Maria letztes Jahr angeschafft hatte. Der sechzehnjährige Moritz machte die

care of the heavy lifting and accounting. Even thirteen-year-old Maria Anna, who was also called Marieche, was learning how to run a business. For now she was only allowed to decorate the tables with flowers or sweep the floors. Marieche was still attending school. Liz and her husband Gerhard occupied two of the rooms on the second floor. Both were the farmers in the family who took care of the animals and the fields. Anton, now thirty-five years old, had taken over the blacksmith business for Macken and neighboring villages. He often boasted about "Hospese Tavern" and invited guests from all over. Anton and his wife lived at her parents' home only a few houses up the road. On Saturday evenings, he played cards with his friends at the "regulars' table" where they loudly enjoyed the beer.

Moritz admired and respected his older brother, but he did not want to become a blacksmith like Anton. Maria didn't mind that Moritz would rather work in the tavern. She understood how the loss of his father had affected him. Moritz helped out in the fields at planting and harvest time. He also looked after the chickens with Marieche and helped his mother in the garden, but he never entered the forge. "Mother, the tavern is my favorite place!" he explained whenever Maria asked about his attitude. Secretly, she couldn't fault him for continuing to avoid the forge. Peter's accident there had been a heavy blow for his young son, Moritz.

"Mother, I'm very worried about Catherine," Liz was just finishing up with the butter churn. "She's been lying around for several days with a long face. She's usually so cheerful and energetic. What could be wrong with her?"

schwere Arbeit und führte die Buchhaltung. Sogar `Marieche,' die dreizehnjährige Maria Anna, lernte wie man ein gutes Geschäft führt. Sie durfte aber vorläufig nur die Tische schmücken oder den Boden kehren. Liz und ihr Mann Gerhard bewohnten zwei Zimmer im oberen Stock. Gerhard war Bauer, und die Beiden pflegten die Felder und das Vieh. Anton, jetzt fünfunddreißig Jahre alt, wurde der amtliche Schmied Mackens und den umliegenden Dörfern. Er prahlte oft von Hospese Wirtschaft und lud Gäste von überall ein. Anton und seine Frau wohnten bei ihren Eltern nur drei Häuser entfernt. An Samstagsabenden spielte er mit seinen Freunden am Stammtisch Karten. Es wurde dann immer laut, als sie sich mit Bier und Würstchen austobten.

Moritz bewunderte und ehrte seinen älteren Bruder, aber er wollte selbst kein Schmied werden. Es machte Maria nichts aus, daß Moritz sich lieber in der Wirtschaft behilflich machte. Moritz half auf den Feldern beim Pflanzen und der Ernte. Er versorgte auch die Hühner und half seiner Mutter im Garten, aber er wollte nichts mit der Schmiede zu tun haben, weil dort sein Vater sein Leben verlor. „Mutter, die Wirtschaft ist meine Lieblingssache!" erklärte er, wann immer Maria sich nach seiner Gesinnung erkundigte. Heimlich konnte sie es ihm nicht übel nehmen. Peters Unfall in der Schmiede war ein schwerer Schlag für den jungen Moritz gewesen.

„Mutter, ich mache mir Sorgen um Catharina," Liz war gerade mit dem Butterfaß fertig. „Sie liegt schon Tagelang herum mit einem langen Gesicht. Sie war doch sonst immer so munter. Was könnte bloß los sein?"

"Liz, I wasn't supposed to tell anyone, but now I can't keep this secret to myself anymore." Liz looked up in surprise. "A few months ago Alois Schmitz attacked Catherine. She fought back, but he raped her anyway. She was so embarrassed that she made me promise not to tell anyone."

"My God, Mother! We can't simply forget something like that or keep it a secret," screamed Liz.

"Listen to me, Liz. If I had said anything about this, Anton and Moritz and perhaps your husband Gerhard would have become very angry. They probably would have beaten up Alois, and who knows what would have come of that. Catherine did not want this, so she dealt with the situation in her own way. We both hoped for the best. Unfortunately, the best did not happen," said Maria with a sad face.

"What do you mean, Mother?"

"Catherine is pregnant!"

"Mother, what are we going to do now? The villagers are sometimes very cruel. Rumors are going to be spread all over!" Liz meant well, but Maria flared up.

"If these farmers can't be a little understanding, I don't want to have anything more to do with them. We have all survived so many hard times together. I'm going to depend on the good will of the Mackeners!" Surprised by her own outburst, Maria started to calm down. "We'll manage somehow."

„Liz, ich sollte eigentlich garnichts sagen, aber jetzt kann ich das Geheimnis nicht mehr einhalten." Liz schaute Maria erstaunt an. „Vor paar Monaten hat Schmitze Alois sie angegriffen. Er ließ sie nicht los und vergewaltigte Catharina. Sie schämte sich so sehr, daß ich ihr versprechen mußte, nichts zu sagen."

„Mein Gott, Mutter! So was kann man doch nicht einfach vergessen und verheimlichen!" schrie Liz.

„Hör mir gut zu, Liz. Wenn ich etwas davon gesagt hätte, wären Anton und Moritz und vielleicht auch dein Mann Gerhard, sehr böse geworden. Sie hätten wahrscheinlich Alois verprügelt, und wer weiß, wie sich das abgespielt hätte. So was wollte Catharina vermeiden. Sie und ich haben heimlich auf das Beste gehofft. Leider ist das Beste nicht gekommen." Maria machte ein trauriges Gesicht.

„Wie meinst du das, Mutter?"

„Catharina ist schwanger!"

„Mutter, was machen wir denn jetzt? Die Dorfleute sind manchmal sehr gefühllos. Überall werden Gerüchte verbreitet!" Liz meinte es gut, aber Maria flammte auf.

„Wenn die Bauern kein Verständnis aufbringen können, dann will ich auch nichts mehr mit ihnen zu tun haben. Wir haben doch schon so viele schlimme Zeiten zusammen überlebt. Ich verlasse mich auf die Mackener!" Maria beruhigte sich wieder.

The next three weeks passed very slowly. Liz and Maria took turns caring for the very ill Catherine. She didn't want to eat or drink and got progressively weaker. One early December morning, Catherine begged in a weak voice, "Mother, Liz, please come help me."

Both stormed up to the bed where Catherine was lying in a pool of blood. "Hurry Liz, go get Luz!" screamed Maria. "She's lost a lot of blood already."

Maria rocked her daughter Catherine in her arms. Liz came back with a cup of tea. "Luz will come as soon as she can. She's also going to bring the village doctor. Here, Catt, take a sip of tea," but Catherine refused it weakly.

Soon they heard Luz coming upstairs. "The doctor is busy somewhere else. Let me see what's going on with Catherine," Luz took one look at her and shook her head in despair. "She's already lost so much blood!" Suddenly Maria felt Catherine go limp in her arms. Carefully, she laid Catherine back on the pillow, got up and stood rooted to floor. Luz checked Catherine again. There was a moment of deathly silence. Quietly, Liz started to cry. Luz stared helplessly at the body.

Luz quickly came to her senses and embraced Maria, "Come on, you two! There is nothing we can do now. Catherine has been relieved of her suffering. We're going to the kitchen to have a cup of coffee. Let's talk about a good future of the rest of your children, Liz, Anton, Moritz and Marieche. Then we will make plans for an especially nice funeral. Come!"

Die nächsten drei Wochen gingen langsam voran. Entweder Liz oder Maria pflegten die kranke Catharina sorgfältig. Sie wollte nichts essen und wurde immer schwächer. An einem frühen Dezembermorgen rufte Catharina mit einer schwachen Stimme, „Mutter, Liz, bitte hilf mir doch."

Beide stürmten ins Zimmer, wo Catharina im Bett blutete. „Schnell, Liz, geh Luzille holen!" brüllte Maria. „Sie hat so viel Blut verloren."

Maria schaukelte Catharina in ihren Armen. Liz kam mit einer Tasse Tee zurück, „Luz kommt gleich. Sie bringt auch den Arzt mit. Hier, Catt, trink doch ein Schlückchen Tee." Aber Catharina lehnte es schwach ab.

Bald kam Luz die Treppe herauf. „Der Arzt ist woanders beschäftigt. Laß mal sehn was mit Catharina los ist." Luz schüttelte verzweifelt den Kopf. „Sie hat schon zu viel Blut verloren!" Maria spürte wie Catharina auf einmal schlaff in ihrer Umarmung wurde. Sie legte Catherina zurück aufs Bett, stand auf und blieb wie verwurzelt stehn. Leise fing Liz zu weinen an. Luz untersuchte Catherina nochmal, aber sie erstarrte.

Luzille besann sich und umarmte Maria. „Kommt, ihr zwei! Hier ist im Moment nichts zu machen. Catharina ist von ihren Leiden befreit. Wir gehen in die Küche und machen uns eine Tasse Kaffee. Dann sprechen wir von der Zukunft deiner übrigen Kindern Liz, Anton, Moritz und Marieche. Danach machen wir Pläne auf eine besonders schöne Beerdigung. Komm!"

Slowly, laboriously, the three women made their way down the stairs. Moritz looked up in surprise as they stumbled into the kitchen. He was in front of the stove getting ready to prepare the soup for tonight's "Special" in the restaurant. "How weird those three look," he thought but didn't say anything.

"Moritz!" Maria was only able to whisper.

"Mother! What is the matter? You three are scaring me."

"Moritz, Catherine is dead!" whispered Liz. Luz confirmed this with a nod of the head.

For a moment total silence filled the house. Holding the ladle in the air, Moritz's hand stopped moving. He felt a shudder run down his spine, and goosebumps form on his skin. Finally, Luz spoke, "Come sit down with us at the table, Moritz. Come here, and we will predict the future for you."

Moritz felt a new tingling sensation raise more goosebumps. The scene seemed surreal. He was eighteen, upstairs was his dead sister, and here in the kitchen three women wanted to predict his future! This scene was simply impossible, but he couldn't tear himself away. "Let me put a fresh pot of coffee on. Mother, you know it's impossible to predict the future," he declared.

"I don't know anything!" Maria agreed gently with Moritz. "Liz and Luz don't know anything either! But here we sit, and we want to explain your life. Wouldn't it at least be interesting to listen?"

Langsam schleppten sich die drei Frauen die Treppe herunter. Moritz schaute verwundert mit seinen lustigen Augen auf. Er stand vor dem Küchenherd und wollte gerade die Suppe für die Wirtschaft vorbereiten, als sie in die Küche kamen. „Wie sieht ihr drei Weiber denn aus?" dachte er, aber er äußerte sich nicht.

„Moritz!" konnte Maria nur sagen.

„Mutter! Was ist los? Ihr Drei macht mir ja Angst."

„Moritz, Catharina ist tot!" flüsterte Liz. Luz bestätigte es mit einem Kopfnicken.

Momentan wurde es mucksmäuschenstill im Haus. Die Hand von Moritz hielt den Kochlöffel in der Luft. Ein Schauder lief ihm über seinen Rücken. Endlich sagte Luz etwas, „Setz dich bei uns an den Tisch, Moritz. Komm her, und wir werden dir deine Zukunft voraussagen."

Moritz spürte Gänsehaut auf seinen Armen. Es war einfach zu unheimlich. Er war achtzehn, oben lag seine tote Schwester, und hier in der Küche wollten drei Frauen seine Zukunft voraussagen! So was gibt es doch nicht! Er konnte sich aber nicht wegreißen. „Laß mich den Kaffee aufstellen. Mutter, du weißt doch, daß man unmöglich die Zukunft voraussagen kann," sagte er nüchtern.

„Ich weiß garnichts!" redete sie Moritz sanft zu. „Liz und Luz wissen garnichts! Aber hier sitzen wir und wollen dir dein Leben erklären. Wäre es nicht interessant uns wenigstens zuzuhören?"

Moritz sensed the goosebumps at the back of his neck again. Then he placed the coffeepot on the table and got the cups out before he took a seat. For a long while, only the stirring of the sugar spoons against the cups could be heard. Frantically Moritz thought, "Somebody say something!" But no one wanted to start talking.

Suddenly Maria said, "Moritz, life is good. One of these days you will get married."

"And your wife will probably have six or seven children," declared Liz.

"And the 'Hospese Tavern' will make you a rich man," added Luz for good measure.

Astonished, Moritz asked, "And will my wife be beautiful?"

Liz said, "Moritz, Beauty is a matter of personal taste. You can select a pretty girl for yourself. We can't help you with that. We also don't have the right to tell you her name."

"Good, then tell me more about the children. Are they all going to die like my little brothers?" Moritz had heard the stories about the horrible deaths of Balthasar, Philip, Johann, Margaretha and Lorenz. He didn't want anything like that to happen to his future family. In his lifetime, he had not experienced such a disaster, but the tiny graves in the cemetery reminded him of the possibility of those things. Sometimes in the tavern, visitors from the cities talked about terrible events in the outside world. Even in America, where nothing

Moritz spürte die Gänsehaut wieder im Nacken. Dann setzte er die Kaffeekanne auf den Tisch und holte Tassen, ehe er sich hinsetzte. Eine lange Weile hörte man nur das Rühren der Zuckerlöffel in den Tassen. Moritz dachte, „Sagt doch etwas, ihr Drei!" aber niemand wollte anfangen.

Plötzlich sprach Maria, „Moritz, das Leben ist gut! Eines Tages wirst du heiraten."

„Und deine Frau bekommt sechs oder sieben Kinder," fügte Liz dazu.

„Und die `Hospese Wirtschaft' wird aus dir einen reichen Mann machen," erklärte Luz. Alle Drei schienen ernst zu sein.

Erstaunt fragte Moritz, „Wird meine Frau auch schön sein?"

Liz sagte, „Moritz, Schönheit ist Geschmacksache. Du kannst dir ja eine Schöne aussuchen. Dabei können wir nicht helfen. Wir haben auch kein Recht dir den Namen zu verraten."

„Gut, dann erzähl' mir noch mehr über die Kinder. Werden sie sterben wie meine Geschwister?" Moritz hatte die schrecklichen Geschichten von Balthasar, Philip, Johann, Margaretha und Lorenz gehört. Er wollte so was Schlimmes nicht mitmachen. In seinem Leben hatte er noch nie so etwas erlebt, aber die kleinen Gräber auf dem Kirchhof erinnerten ihn an die Möglichkeit solcher Dinge. Manchmal hörte er durch Besucher in der Wirtschaft von den schlimmen Ereignissen in der Außenwelt. Sogar in Amerika, wo

bad was ever supposed to happen, people were killing each other in a civil war. Moritz was already worrying about his unborn children.

Lucille cleared her throat. "Moritz, anything can happen. We could have another epidemic. We could have more wars. Blood could be running in the streets, and you could break your finger while picking your nose. On the other hand, we could also have peace and health. Your family could become rich. Your descendants could travel all over the world and become important people. Why not think about these good things?"

Maria cheered up a bit as she spoke, "Yes, Moritz, I have already buried five babies, and now my adult daughter is lying dead in her bed. But I have you and Marieche. Your father also gave me Liz and Anton. I cannot afford to despair. I cannot deny my wonderful living family or neglect you. You are my son, and you are strong enough to establish your own family and provide for them. Don't be afraid. The future is in your own hands."

"Gerhard and I will always stand by you," promised Liz. Liz had no children. Lucille and Maria had often discussed the possibility that Liz became barren because she had seen too many deaths in her family.

Suddenly the door burst open with a bang. "Hey, what are you sitting around for?" yelled Marieche, the energetic teenager. She had been feeding the chickens and gathering the eggs.

nichts Schlimmes passieren sollte, gab es einen Bürgerkrieg. Moritz war jetzt schon über seine noch nicht geborene Kinder besorgt.

Luzille räusperte sich, „Moritz, es kann alles passieren. Es könnte wieder eine Seuche kommen, Es könnte Kriege geben. Blut könnte auf den Straßen fließen, und man könnte sich den Finger in der Nase abbrechen. Andererseits, könnte es auch Frieden geben, und Gesundheit. Deine Familie könnte gesund und reich werden. Deine Nachahmen könnten auf der ganzen Welt herumfahren und wichtige Leute werden. Warum denken wir nicht an das Beste?"

Maria heiterte ein wenig auf, „Ja, Moritz, ich habe schon fünf Kinderchen begraben, und nun liegt meine erwachseneTochter tot in ihrem Bett! Aber ich habe dich und Marieche. Dein Vater gab mir Liz und Anton. Ich kann doch nicht meine wunderbare lebendige Familie verstoßen oder vernachlässigen! Du bist mein Sohn, und du bist stark genug deine eigene Familie zu gründen und gut versorgen. Hab keine Angst! Die Zukunft liegt in deinen Händen."

„Gerhard und ich stehen dir auch immer bei," versprach Liz. Liz hatte keine Kinder bekommen. Luzille und Maria hatten die Möglichkeit besprochen, daß Liz zu viele Kinder hatte sterben gesehn. Vielleicht wurde sie deshalb unfruchtbar.

Plötzlich schlug jemand die Tür auf, „He, was ist mit euch allen los?" platzte das energische Marieche in die Küche. Sie kam gerade vom Hof wo sie die Hühner fütterte. Sie hatte ein Körbchen

She was carrying a basket of eggs. "Brr, it's cold outside. We still have a lot of chores to do. Why are you all sitting here?"

"Please sit down with us and be quiet," warned her mother. "Catherine is dead."

"What! I don't believe you!" Marieche started to scream and run toward the stairs.

"I said, sit down!" hissed Maria between clenched teeth.

Marieche set the egg basket down and quickly grabbed a towel. Then she sat down next to her mother. Tears welled up in her eyes. "Does Anton know what has happened?"

"If you promise not to make a hysterical fuss and upset his pregnant wife, I will let you go tell them." Maria's voice had gotten gentle again.

Marieche calmed down a little. "May I go upstairs first. I want to see Catherine for myself." Marieche knew nothing about the cause of this death. "How can a healthy young woman die so suddenly?" she wondered. No one answered her question.

Maria gave her permission, "Okay, go upstairs for a few minutes. Then you'll wash your face and comb your hair before you're going to Anton's house."

Liz took control of the topic. "So, Moritz, now you know the situation. We women are going to discuss the funeral. You can go

Eier in der Hand. „Brr, es ist kalt draußen. Wir haben noch viel Arbeit heute. Warum sitzt ihr denn alle hier?"

„Bitte setz dich zu uns und sei still," mahnte ihre Mutter. „Catharina ist tot."

„Was? Das glaube ich dir nicht!" Marieche fing zu schreien an.

„Ich habe gesagt, setz' dich!" zichte Maria durch ihre Zähne.

Marieche legte den Eierkorb auf das Brett und nahm schnell ein Handtuch. Dann setzte sie sich neben ihre Mutter. Tränen standen dick in ihren Augen. „Weiß Anton, was passiert ist?"

„Wenn du mir versprichst, ihn und seine schwangere Frau nicht hysterisch aufzuregen, darfst du ihnen Bescheid sagen," Marias Stimme war wieder sanft geworden.

Marieche beruhigte sich ein wenig. „Darf ich erst 'rauf gehn? Ich will Catharina selbst sehn." Marieche wußte nichts von der Ursache des Todes. „Wie kann eine kerngesunde junge Frau so plötzlich sterben?" wunderte sie sich heimlich.

Maria erlaubte ihr, „Gut, geh ein paar Minuten ,rauf. Dann wäschst du dir das Gesicht und kämmst dir die Haare, ehe du zu Antons gehst."

Liz nahm die Leitung des Themas. „Also Moritz, nun weißt du Bescheid! Wir Frauen besprechen jetzt die Beerdigung. Du darfst

back to cooking your soup for the restaurant. 'Hospese Tavern' needs the strong hand of Moritz Hammes."

dich wieder mit deiner Suppe beschäftigen. Die Wirtschaft braucht die feste Hand des Moritz Hammes."

1873 to the present

The Interval

Moritz Hammes married Barbara Pies from the village of Dommershausen. They became the parents of seven children who lived long and healthy lives.

Magdalena, born in 1876, moved to Koblenz to be a maid in a wealthy family. She eventually married Jakob Sprink. They had three children, Peter, Katherine (Ketta) and Johann.

Katherine, born in 1878, married Nikola Arenz, a stone mason. They remained childless and lived most of their lives in her home village of Macken.

. 1965 Maria Küppers, nee Hammes, Leni Dott, Ketta Dott, nee Sprink and Tilli Miller, nee Küppers

Barbara, born in 1880, also moved to Koblenz to be a maid and governess to a wealthy family. She eventually married Joseph Schmitz. They had three daughters and a son, also named Joseph. The two oldest daughters married Jewish

1873 to the present

Zwischendurch

Moritz Hammes heiratete Barbara Pies aus Dommershausen. Sie wurden die Eltern von sieben Kindern, die alle lang und gesund lebten.

Magdalena, 1878 geboren, zog nach Kobenz, wo sie als Dienstmädchen bei einer reichen Familie arbeitete. Sie heiratete Jakob Sprink. She hatten drei Kinder, Peter, Katharina und Johann.

Katherine, 1878 geboren, heiratete Nikola Arenz, einen Maurer. Sie hatten keine Kinder und wohnten den grössten Teil ihres Lebens in ihrem Geburtsort Macken.

Barbara, 1830 geboren, zog auch nach Koblenz, wo sie als Kindermädchen einer reichen Familie wirkte. Sie heiratete Joseph Schmitz und führten ein Lebens-mittelgeschäft. Sie hatten drei Töchter und einen Sohn. Die älteren zwei Mädchen heirateten Juden und wanderten nach Amerika aus als sie Hitler's Absichten bemerkten. Eine

. *Katherine and Nikola Arenz, 50th Anniversary*

men and emigrated when they became aware of Hitler's intentions. One of their daughters, Gerda, married a German pilot who became a casualty of World War II, and Joseph, their only son, was killed early in the war, leaving a grieving widow and a baby daughter behind. Joseph died of a stroke shortly after his son's death. Barbara maintained a small grocery store until World War two forced her out.

Peter, probably born in 1882, eventually moved to a northern German city. When the Iron Curtain was built, he was on the other side. It was a long time before any of his siblings would be able to visit him again.

In 1885, Wilhelm was born. He moved to Frankfurt and married a woman there who gave him twin sons.

Moritz, born in 1886, was then assumed to be the last child of Moritz and Barbara. Very little is known of him in the family lore. Perhaps he stayed in Macken to help his parents with the tavern.

Maria was a surprise baby in September 1888. She was a dear little quiet one who was adored by her older sisters. She grew into a strapping youngster and was sent to Koblenz at age fourteen to be a maid in a rich family. She worked there until she beame a single mother at age twenty-one.

In April 1889, Maria Korzilius, passed away in the knowledge that her posterity would be in the good hands of another Maria.

Tochter, Gerda, heiratete einen Flieger der im Zweiten Weltkrieg abgeschossen wurde. Ihr einziger Sohn Joseph, fiel früh im Krieg. Er hinterliess eine trauernde Frau und ein Töchterchen, Ingrid. Barbaras Ehemann, Joseph, starb kurz nach dem Tod seines Sohnes, auch namens Joseph. Ihr Geschäft wurde wegen des Krieges geschlossen.

Peter, wahrscheinlich 1882 geboren, zog nach einer Stadt im Norden Deutschlands. Nachdem der Eiserne Vorhang gebaut wurde, durften seine Geschwister ihn eine lange Zeit nicht besuchen.

In 1885 kam Wilhelm auf die Welt. Er zog nach Frankfurt, und heiratete dort eine Frau, die ihm Zwillingsjungen gab.

Moritz, 1886 geboren, sollte eigentlich das letzte Kind von Moritz und Barbara sein. Ganz wenig ist von ihm in der Familie bekannt. Vielleicht blieb er in Macken um seinen Eltern in der Wirtschaft zu helfen.

Maria kam im September 1888 auf die Welt. Ein liebes Kind, vergöttert von ihren älteren Schwestern, sie wuchs kräftig heran. Mit vierzehn wurde sie nach Koblenz in eine reiche Familie geschickt. Dort arbeitete sie als Dienstmädchen bis sie mit einundzwanzig ein uneheliches Kind bekam.

Im April 1889 starb Maria Korzilius in dem Gedanken, daß ihre Nachkunft in den guten Händen einer anderen Maria lag.

1909

Martha in Macken

Moritz and Barbara Hammes had managed well with their seven children. Except for Katherine, they all moved away to the cities. Their sons, Peter, Wilhelm and Moritz went to work in Berlin. Magdalene, Barbara and Maria lived and worked in Koblenz.

Now in his old age, Moritz wanted to enjoy the peace and quiet of being in his tavern where Katherine was helping him. Barbara was in the yard feeding the chickens.

Suddenly Barbara called to them, "Moritz, Katt! Maria just arrived for a visit! What could be bringing her to Macken in the middle of the year?"

"You know how young girls are, Barb. Sometimes here; sometimes there. They simply can't find a place to rest."

"Hello, Maria, come here for a big kiss! What brings you to Macken?" Barbara greeted her youngest daughter. "Come, let's go into the kitchen and make some coffee."

"Mother, sit down, I have something important to tell you." Maria had an embarrassed look on her face. "Mother, I think I'm going to have a baby in December."

"Oh my God! Is the father going to marry you?"

1909

Martha in Macken

Moritz und Barbara Hammes hatten ihre eigenen sieben Kinder gut untergebracht. Ausser Katherine, zogen alle in eine Stadt. Die Jungen, Peter, Wilhelm und Moritz arbeiteten in Berlin oder Frankfurt. Magdalene, Barbara und Maria wohnten in Koblenz.

Jetzt wollte Moritz in seinem Alter die Ruhe geniessen, und nur an seine Wirtschaft denken. Moritz war gerade mit Katherine in der Wirtschaft beschäftigt als Barbara im Hof die Hühner fütterte.

Plötzlich rief Barbara zu Moritz, „Maria ist auf Besuch! Was bringt sie denn mitten im Jahr nach Macken?"

„Du weisst ja wie so'n junges Mädchen ist, Barb. Einmal da, einmal hier. Die haben einfach keine Ruhe."

„Hallo Marieche, komm her für e'n dicke Kuss! Was bringt dich denn nach Macken?" rief Barbara. „Komm wir gehn in die Küche und machen Kaffee."

„Mutter, setz dich. Ich muss dir was erzählen." Maria machte ein ziemlich beschämtes Gesicht. „Mutter, ich glaube ich bekomme im Dezember ein Kind."

„Um Gotteswillen! Will der Mann dich heiraten?"

Maria shook her head. She whispered, "No. His family is against it. Carl loves me, but his father threatened to disinherit him if he marries me."

"Maria, what kind of people are they?"

"Mother, they are very rich wine growers in Mesenich on the Mosel. They think I'm too poor and not good enough for their son who will inherit the vineyards if he obeys them. He promised to pay every month if you could raise the baby for us."

"You can depend on us, Maria. Your father will probably make a face, but I'll find a way to turn him around. What do your employers think about this situation?" Barbara was very worried about her youngest daughter who was crying softly.

"They don't know anything about it. As soon as it becomes obvious, I'll quit my job. For a while I can live with my sisters, Magda or Barbara. When the baby is ready to be born, I'll go to the maternity hospital in Mayen. Then I will come back here to Macken and bring you the baby. After my convalescence, I'll go back to Koblenz. I'm sure I'll find another job as a maid or a governess."

Despite her unhappy situation Maria was aware of her own abilities and self-confident about her decisions.

"So, shall we plan on raising the child here in Macken with us?" Barbara wanted to know.

Maria schüttelte den Kopf. Leise flüsterte sie, „Nein. Seine Familie ist dagegen. Carl liebt mich, aber sein Vater hat ihn schon mit Enterben gedroht."

"Maria, was sind das denn für Leute?" fragte Barbara.

"Mutter, sie sind sehr reiche Winzer aus Mesenich an der Mosel. Sie meinen, ich wäre als armes Mädchen nicht gut genug für ihren Sohn der auch mal Winzer werden soll. Er hat mir monatliches Geld für euch versprochen wenn ihr unser Kind erzieht."

„Du kannst dich auf uns verlassen, Maria. Dein Vater macht vielleicht ein Gesicht, aber ich werd' schon mit ihm fertig werden. Was denken denn deine Leute von der Geschichte?" Barbara machte sich Sorgen um ihre jüngste Tochter die weinend vor ihr stand.

„Die wissen noch nichts davon. Sobald sie was merken, kündige ich meine Stelle. Ich kann eine zeitlang bei meinen Schwestern, Magda oder Barbara, verweilen. Wenn das Kind kommt, gehe ich zum Mutterheim in Mayen. Dann komme ich heim und bringe dir das Kind. Wenn ich mich erholt habe, gehe ich wieder nach Koblenz. Ich werde wohl eine andere Stelle als Dienstmädchen finden."

Trotz ihrer unglücklichen Umständen war Maria selbstbewusst und zuversichtlich.

„Also sollen wir denn das Kind erziehen?" wollte Barbara wissen.

"Yes, Mother, you have a lot of experience raising children. All seven of us are educated and healthy. I'm sure you'll take good care of my baby. Do you think that Father will agree to my plan?"

"Yes, he is already bored around here because there aren't any children in the house. He keeps himself busy with the tavern, but in the evenings he would love to have a small child climb into his lap. The other day he even complained that Katherine and Nikola can't have any children. You know that she had to suffer that hysterectomy a few years ago." For a moment, Barbara became sad.

"What are you women talking so much about?" Moritz walked briefly into the kitchen for a cup of coffee.

"Oh, Moritz, you don't always have to mix yourself into women's talk. But now that you've asked, you're going to have to listen. Maria is pregnant. She will get her baby in December." Barbara had become defiant.

For a moment Moritz was completely quiet. Then he left.

"Maria, don't worry. It will take him a little while till he has digested this situation," Barbara assured her daughter.

Barbara and Moritz adored little Martha. Also, Auntie Katt carried the baby in her arms to the garden to show her all the pretty flowers growing there. Martha was well taken care of.

„Ja, Mutter, ihr habt ja gute Erfahrung mit Kindern. Wir sind alle sieben gut erzogen und gesund. Du wirst auch mein Kindchen gut betreuen. Meinst du, dass Vater auch damit einverstanden ist?"

„Ja, es wird ihm jetzt schon langweilig, weil keine Kinder mehr im Haus sind. Er ist ja meistens mit der Wirtschaft beschäftigt, aber abends wäre er doch froh wenn ein kleines Kind auf seinen Schoss klettern würde. Er hat schon gemeckert, das Katherine und Nikola keine Kinder bekommen, aber sie musste doch die schwere Hysterektomie durchmachen." Barbara wurde momentan traurig.

„Was schwätzt ihr Weiber denn so viel?" Moritz kam gerade in die Küche und schenkte sich eine Tasse Kaffee ein.

„Ach Moritz, du brauchst dich nicht immer in Frauensachen einmischen. Aber wenn du schon fragst, dann musst du es auch jetzt schon erfahren. Maria bekommt im Dezember ein Kind," antwortete Barbara mit Mut.

Moritz war momentan still. Dann ging er wieder hinaus.

„Maria, es wird ihm ein Weile nehmen, bis er diese Neuigkeit verdaut hat," versicherte Barbara ihrer Tochter.

Barbara und Moritz vergötterten die kleine Martha. Auch Tante Katt trug sie oft auf dem Arm in den Garten wo sie dem Kind die schönen Blumen zeigte. Martha hatte es gut in Macken.

In the Spring of 1912 Moritz became very ill. A seemingly unimportant injury to his right hand didn't heal and became infected. The infection went into his bloodstream. By June, he appeared to be dying. In his fever he recalled his mother, Luz and Liz and how they predicted his future. Now he had a large family that was gradually moving out into the world.

All his grown children with their families came to visit him as he lay dying. Magda brought young Peter and little Katherine. Barbara brought her three little daughters, Lizbet, Maria and Gerda. Maria brought her husband, Hans Küppers and his little son, Hans.

Moritz told them the stories about his mother Maria. Then he wished them all much success in life, but he knew that he would not recover. Shortly after the visit, he died.

Grandma Barbara and Aunt Katt continued to take good care of little Martha as she grew into a beautiful young lady. When she completed her school years, she was sent to work for a family in the city.

Around 1930, Martha Hammes, visiting her father's family vineyards.

Leider wurde Moritz Anfang 1912 sehr krank. Eine unwichtige kleine Verletzung an der rechten Hand wollte nicht heilen und wurde entzündet. Die Infektion ging ihm ins Blut. Im Juni lag er im Sterben. Er dachte zurück, wie seine Mutter, Luz und Liz ihm die Zukunft damals schilderten. Jetzt hatte er eine grosse Familie, die sich langsam in der Welt verbreitete.

Alle seine erwachsene Kinder kamen mit ihren Familien den kranken Familienvater zu besuchen. Magda brachte ihren kleinen Peter und ihr Katherienchen. Barbara brachte ihre drei Töchterchen, Lizbet, Maria und Gerda. Maria brachte ihren Mann, Hans Küppers und dessen Sohn Hans.

Moritz erzählte ihnen von seiner Mutter Maria. Dann wünschte er ihnen viel Erfolg im Leben, aber er selbst war nicht mehr zu retten. Kurz nach dem Besuch, starb er.

Grossmutter Barbara und Tante Katt versorgten die kleine Martha bis sie in eine bildschöne junge Frau wuchs. Als sie mit der Schule fertig war, wurde sie in die Stadt zu einer Familie als Kindermädchen geschickt.

1935, Martha Hammes, auf der Hochzeit ihrer Schwester Tilli.

The children of Maria and Hans Küppers, Leni, Tilli and Jupp, occasionally visited in Macken between the two world wars. There was always plenty of food, even though there was no electricity, running water or indoor toilets. After only a few days in Macken, Maria and the children were always ready to return to their beautiful apartment in the city. The children grew up in Koblenz. After Martha moved out and Grandmother Barbara died, the old homestead in Macken was forgotten until after World War II. Only Katherine and her husband Nikola stayed in the old house.

Auch die Kinder von Maria und Hans, Leni, Tilli und Jupp, durften ab und zu ihre Ferien nach dem Ersten Weltkrieg auf dem Land in Macken verbringen. Dort gab es immer genug zu Essen, selbst wenn es keine Wasserleitungen, Elektrizität oder richtige Toiletten im Haus gab. Nach einigen Tagen in Macken, wollte Maria mit den Kindern immer wieder in the Stadt, wo sie ihre schöne Wohnung in einem modernen Wohnhaus hatte zurück. Die Kinder wurden in der Stadt Koblenz gross. Das alte Heim of dem Land wurde bis zum Zweiten Weltkrieg vergessen. Nur Katherine und Nikola bewohnten das alte Haus.

Book Two

1947 Marianne in Macken

Zweites Buch

. 1968 Maria Küppers makes her second trip to the United States, Maria macht ihre zweite Reise nach Amerika

1945

Maria and Marianne

"Oma!" I yelled as soon as I noticed her on the train platform. Oma was my much loved grandmother, Maria Küppers. Now she lived in the home of her birth in Macken in the Hunsrück mountains. She had come to pick up my mother and me in Burgen where the train stopped. One year earlier, when the bombings of World War II became intolerable in Koblenz, my mother and I had fled to St. Wolfgang in Austria. Oma and Opa refused to leave Koblenz. I even heard her declare that she had survived the first world war in her apartment, and now she planned to survive the second one, with or without her head! When the war ended, I expected to be able to go back to Oma and Opa in Koblenz and move in with them in their comfortable city apartment, but they did not live there anymore.

After our happy "Hellos" we climbed onto the oxcart that would take us up the mountain to Macken. My mother, whom I called "Mutti" was still very weak from an infection in her throat and the stress of a terrible trip from St. Wolfgang. I was not well, either. My eyelids kept sticking together, making it difficult for me to see. Poverty-stricken and godforsaken, we were going to arrive in Macken one hour later.

As the oxcart rattled on, Oma looked at me with a worried face, "Marianne, what happened to your eyes?"

1945

Maria und Marianne

„Oma!" brüllte ich, sobald ich sie auf dem Bahnsteig sah.
Oma war meine beliebte Grossmutter Maria Küppers. Sie wohnte
jetzt in ihrem Geburtshaus in Macken auf dem Hunsrück und kam
uns am Zug in Burgen abholen. Ein Jahr vorher, als die Bomben-
angriffe über Koblenz im zweiten Weltkrieg zu furchtbar wurden,
flohen meine Mutti und ich nach St. Wolfgang in Österreich. Oma
und Opa blieben aber in der Stadt. Oma hat immer gesagt, daß die
den ersten Weltkrieg in ihrer eigenen Wohnung überlebt hat, und
jetzt wird sie auch den Zweiten überleben, mit oder ohne Kopf! Als
der Krieg zu Ende kam, habe ich gemeint, wir könnten wieder bei
Oma und Opa in Koblenz einziehen, aber sie waren nicht mehr in
der schönen Wohnung.

Nach unserer frohen Begrüssung wurden wir mit einer
Ochsenkarre nach Macken gefahren. Mutti war noch sehr schwach
von einer Infektion im Hals und den Strapazen der Heimfahrt von St.
Wolfgang. Meine Augenlider klebten immer zusammen, was mir
Schwierigkeiten machte. Armselig, krank und gottverlassen sollten
wir eine Stunde später in Macken ankommen.

„Mariannche, was ist denn mit deinen Augen los?" Meine
Oma schaute mich unterwegs besorgt an.

"Mutti said that the coal dust got into my eyes. Now I have to pry them open with my fingers if I want to look at something," I explained matter-of-factly.

"Coal dust? How in the world did you get near coal dust?"

My mother quickly jumped in with the explanation. "Our trip from St. Wolfgang took three days on different trains. There were no passenger cars. That's why we had to ride in cattle cars or on top of coal carriers. We had to climb up and down, and even go on foot when a train couldn't cross a river because of a destroyed bridge. Mother, it was a horrible trip."

"Yes, and I'm glad that Uncle Jupp came to get us. Mutti was very sick in St. Wolfgang, and I was scared that she would die," I added to the story.

Oma comforted me, "You poor child. We'll take care of your eyes, and your mother will also get her health back here in Macken. We have enough to eat, and she will get plenty of rest in our home. After all, your mother is my child."

"My mother is not a child," I objected.

"Sure, I know that, sweet Marianne, but she was a child once, and now she is a grown-up, but I'm still her mother no matter what. That's why I'm going to take good care of her," answered Oma.

„Mutti hat gesagt, daß der Kohlenstaub mir in die Augen gegangen ist. Jetzt muss ich sie mit den Fingern aufmachen wenn ich etwas sehn will," erklärte ich ganz nüchtern.

„Kohlenstaub? Wie bist du denn an Kohlenstaub gekommen?"

Meine Mutti gab schnell Antwort, „Die Zugfahrt von St. Wolfgang nahm drei Tage. Es gab keine Passagierwagen. Deshalb mussten wir auf Kohlenwagen oder in Viehtransportwagen einen Platz suchen. Wir mussten öfters aus- und einsteigen, und manchmal eine Weile zu Fuss gehn wenn eine Brücke kaputt war. Mutter, es war eine ganz schreckliche Fahrt."

„Ja, ich war froh daß Onkel Jupp uns abgeholt hat. Die Mutti war schwer krank in St. Wolfgang, und ich hatte Angst sie würde sterben," fügte ich zu der Geschichte.

„Du armes Kind. Wir werden dir schon die Augen wieder heilen. Und deine Mutti wird auch wieder in Macken gesund. Wir haben genug zu Essen, und sie kann sich bei uns gut ausruhen. Deine Mutti ist ja mein Kind."

„Meine Mutti ist doch kein Kind," weigerte ich mich.

„Na, das weiß ich doch, Mariannche, aber sie war mal mein Kind, und jetzt ist sie meine erwachsene Tochter. Trotzdem bleibe ich ihre Mutter, und so werde ich sie pflegen," antwortete Oma.

My mother smiled, "Mother, I'm not going to stay in Macken very long. In a small village I won't have any opportunity to earn money. Gerda has invited me to come sew some new clothes out of her old things, but unfortunately her small house does not have enough room for Marianne. Do you think she could stay with you until I can get my own place?"

"Gerda? Do you mean our Gerda, the daughter of my sister Barbara? How is she doing? I remember that she lost her husband and her brother in the war, and now even her father is dead. Does your aunt Barbara also live with her in that small house?" Oma had me sitting on her lap as she wanted to know all about the family Schmitz. "Of course, Marianne can stay with us."

"Yes, on our trip back from St. Wolfgang, Jupp told me all about Gerda and aunt Barbara. They got out of Koblenz just before one of the worst air raids. It's a good thing that Gerda and her husband bought the little vacation house in Burgen before the war. Now it is the only home they still have left, and all the men in their family are dead."

. *1947 Cousins Gerda and Tilli*

100

Meine Mutti lächelte, „Mutter, ich bleibe nicht lange in Macken. In dem kleinen Dorf gibt es für mich keine Gelegenheit Geld zu machen. Gerda hat mich eingeladen um ihr paar neue Kleider aus ihren alten Klamotten zu machen, aber in dem kleinen Häuschen ist leider kein Platz für Marianne. Meinst du, sie könnte vielleicht bei euch bleiben bis ich wieder meine eigene Wohnung kriege?"

„Gerda? Meinst du unsere Gerda, die Tochter meiner Schwester Barbara? Wie geht es ihr eigentlich? Sie hat doch ihren Mann und ihren Bruder im Krieg verloren, und jetzt ist auch ihr Vater tot. Wohnt Tante Bepp bei ihr in dem kleinen Häuschen?" Oma hielt mich immernoch auf dem Schoss als sie sich um die Familie Schmitz erkundigte. "Natürlich kann Marianne bei uns bleiben."

„Ja, auf der Fahrt hat Jupp mir alles von Gerda und Tante Bepp erzählt. Sie kamen gerade noch vor einem schlimmen Angriff aus Koblenz. Gut dass Gerda und ihr Mann sich das Ferienhäuschen in Burgen vor dem Krieg angeschafft hatten. Jetzt ist es die einzige Wohnstätte, die sie noch haben, und alle ihre Männer sind tot."

Gerda, Ingrid & Barbara Schmitz

„Ja, der Krieg hat viel Elend mitgebracht," bemerkte Oma.

My mother's face was very sad. "And my husband is a prisoner of war of the Americans. God only knows where, either in Italy or here in Germany. He can't help me. I have to support myself and my little daughter Marianne now."

"Tilli, you can always depend on us. Marianne will be well taken care of and get healthy again. After the war we also had to leave the city even though our building wasn't destroyed." Oma suddenly had tears in her eyes.

"Why was that? When we arrived at Jupp's place I noticed the strangers in the apartment. How could that happen?" Mutti and Oma looked at each other and shook their heads.

"Tilli, shortly after the stupid bombings stopped, somebody from the authorities took control of our apartment. One room was set aside for Jupp, and one room was supposed to be for Opa and me. The kitchen and the parlor would be assigned to strangers. I couldn't tolerate that, so I called our friend Pete Neuert right away.

With his truck, Pete brought us and our furniture to Macken. I would not have been able to endure sharing my apartment with strangers." I was feeling very sorry for my Oma. I knew how much she cared for her home in Koblenz.

I smiled at her and petted her arm. "Oma, I'm glad you didn't get killed in the war. In St. Wolfgang I was always thinking about you and Opa. Now I can stay with you in Macken. It doesn't matter where we are living as long as we're together again. Are we going to arrive in Macken pretty soon?

Meine Mutti machte ein sehr trauriges Gesicht. „Und mein Mann ist in amerikanischer Gefangenschaft, Gott weiss wo, entweder in Italien oder hier in Deutschland. Er kann mir nicht helfen. Ich muss mich um mich selbst und Marianne besorgen.

„Tilli, du kannst dich in jedem Falle auf uns verlassen. Marianne wird bei uns wieder heil. Nach dem Krieg mussten wir auch die Stadt verlassen obwohl unser Haus nicht getroffen wurde,“ Oma hatte plötzlich Tränen in den Augen.

„Ja, Mutter, warum denn? Als wir bei Jupp ankamen hab ich fremde Leute in der Wohnung gesehn. Wie ist denn so was passiert?“ Mutti und Oma guckten sich einander an.

„Tilli, kurz nachdem die blöde Bomberei aufhörte, kam jemand von der Behörde unsere Wohnung zu beschlagnahmen. Ein Zimmer wurde Jupp genehmigt, und ein Zimmer sollte uns zugewiesen werden. Eine fremde Familie sollte meine Küche und das Wohnzimmer bekommen. Ich konnte das nicht mitmachen, deshalb habe ich direkt unseren Freund, Neuertse Pitt, gerufen.

Mit seinem Kraftwagen hat er uns und unsere Möbel nach Macken gebracht. Ich hätte das Teilen meiner Wohnung mit fremden Leuten nicht ausgehalten.“ Oma tat mir in dem Moment sehr Leid. Ich habe gewusst, wie sehr sie an ihrem Heim in Koblenz hang, und wie sorgfältig sie es pflegte.

Ich lächelte sie an und streichelte ihren Arm, „Oma, ich bin froh, daß du nicht im Krieg gestorben bist. Ich habe in St. Wolfgang immer an dich und Opa gedacht. Jetzt kann ich bei euch bleiben. Es ist ja egal wo wir wohnen. Kommen wir bald in Macken an? Dieser

103

This oxcart is shaking so hard, and besides, I'm hungry," I was jabbering almost to myself.

Oma and Mutti laughed at me. I was glad that I was able to distract them from their serious discussion. The war had matured me at eight years old. My mother and my grandmother were my world, and I didn't want to see them cry anymore.

When we arrived in Macken, Opa helped us down from the oxcart and hugged me very tightly. It was a pleasure to feel his strong arms and smell the familiar pipe tobacco. I started to believe that nothing bad could ever happen again now that I was back with my grandparents.

Wagen wackelt so viel, und ich habe auch Hunger," plabberte ich so vor mich hin.

Oma und Mutti lachten mich aus. Ich war froh, daß ich sie von dem ernsten Thema ablenken konnte. Der Krieg hatte mich mit acht Jahren schon reif gemacht. Meine Mutti und meine Oma waren meine Welt, und ich wollte sie nicht mehr weinen sehn.

In Macken half uns Opa von der Ochsenkarre und drückte mich ganz fest. Es war ein Genuss seine starke Arme und seinen familiären Geruch zu vernehmen. Ich fühlte mich direkt wohl. Jetzt war ich wieder mit meinen beliebten Großeltern, und es konnte nichts Schlimmes mehr passieren.

Despite my tender age of eight years, I was no longer a child; rather, I was a war veteran. I was supposed to be destroyed, but the war was unable to achieve that. My innocent childhood was denied me, but in exchange I got a sober and serious mind.

In Macken, a small village in the Hunsrück mountains, I found a warm, secure, colorful and friendly world that I could never have imagined. My Oma was determined to heal me from the shocks of the war. She started by treating my eyes.

"Oma, what is the matter with my eyes? I can't open them in the mornings. I always have to pull my eyelids open with my fingers when I wake up."

"Marianne, you have conjunctivitis, an infection in your eyes. The sticky stuff is pus. If you hold your face over this bowl full of hot chamomile tea, the infection will be pulled out, and then you'll be able to see again." Oma sounded very assuring. "Here, I'll hang a towel over your head. Then you're going to stay for ten minutes under the towel tent. We'll do this every day."

It took almost two weeks until the pus stopped accumulating in my eyes. Slowly, my eyes began to notice tiny ladybugs and colorful flowers in the garden. These small creatures knew nothing about the war that had devastated the human world. Whenever a red ladybug crawled on my fingers, or a butterfly landed on my shoulders or even a stinging nettle burned my leg, I frolicked in the middle of this natural life.

Trotz meinem zarten Alter von acht Jahren war ich kein kleines Kind mehr; ich war eher ein Kriegsausgedienter. Man hatte mich vernichten wollen, aber das ist denen Krieger nicht gelungen.

Die unschuldige Kindheit ist mir versagt worden, aber dafür bekam ich einen nüchternen Verstand.

In Macken, ein kleines Hunsrück Dorf, fand ich eine warme, sichere, bunte und freundliche Welt, wie ich sie mir niemals vorstellen konnte. Meine Oma nahm sich vor, mich von dem Kriegsschreck abzulenken. Zuerst fing sie an, meine Augen zu behandeln.

„Oma, was ist denn eigentlich mit meinen Augen los? Ich kann sie morgens nicht aufmachen. Ich muss immer mit meinen Fingern die Lider aufziehen. Es gibt doch kein Kohlenstaub hier."

„Marianne, du hast eine Bindehautentzündung. Das Klebzeug ist Eiter. Wenn du dein Gesicht über diese Schüssel mit dem heißen Kamillentee hältst, dann geht die Entzündung weg, und dann kannst du wieder gut sehen," versicherte Oma mich. „Hier, ich hänge ein Handtuch über deinen Kopf. Du bleibst dann zehn Minuten unter dem Kamillenteezelt."

Es dauerte fast zwei Wochen bis keinen Eiter aus meinen Augen kam. Langsam fingen meine Augen an bunte Blümchen und kleine Käfer zu sehen. Diese kleine Lebewesen wussten nichts von dem Krieg, der die Leute so verwüstet hatte. Wenn mir ein rotes Marienkäferchen auf den Fingern krabbelte, ein bunter Schmetterling mir auf die Schulter flog, oder sogar eine Brennessel mich am Bein brannte frohlockte ich in Mitte des Naturlebens.

I had been a scared little girl who used to run randomly in shock. In Macken I gradually developed into an enlightened, self-confident child. Now my life could begin anew because I could see again. Yes, I even noticed that my brave Oma Maria knew exactly how to treat her family.

My mother left two weeks later. She had recovered enough to be able to walk the hour down the mountain from Macken to Burgen. I wanted to go with her, but she explained one more time that Gerda's little vacation house did not have enough room for both of us. Besides, she was planning to go to Koblenz a month later, where she could probably stay with the Merks family.

"Mutti, are the Merks' still alive?" I had already gotten so accustomed to the terrible mortality of people involved in the world war that I was surprised to hear familiar names. Perhaps all our friends were dead.

"Yes, my brother Jupp told me about the Merks'. Annemie, Marie, and Kathie are still living in their old apartment, but Hella has moved to Frankfurt."

Aunt Hella had always been my favorite one of the Merks sisters, "I can still remember that she worked in a butcher shop before the war. She always gave me a big slice of bologna when we went shopping there. Why did she move to Frankfurt?" I was curious about the smallest details. I also acquired the new habit of organizing my thoughts by adding "before the war," or "after the war."

Während dem Krieg war ich ein kleines ängstliches Mädchen, das vor Schrecken kopfüber und schnurstracks irgendwohin rannte, gewesen. Im Frieden der Natur entwickelte ich mich langsam in ein helles selbsbewusstes Kind. Jetzt konnte mein Leben wieder von Neuem anfangen, weil ich wieder sehen konnte. Ja, meine Oma Maria wußte schon wie man eine Familie versorgt.

Zwei Wochen später ging Mutti. Sie war wieder gesund genug, um die Stunde zu Fuss von Macken nach Burgen zu laufen. Ich wollte mit, aber sie erklärte mir nochmal, daß das kleine Häuschen von Gerda nicht genug Platz für uns beide hatte. Außerdem hatte sie vor, nächsten Monat nach Koblenz, wo sie vielleicht bei Familie Merks wohnen könnte, zu fahren.

„Mutti, sind denn die Merkse noch alle am Leben?" Ich hatte mich schon an die schreckliche Sterblichkeit der Menschen in einem Krieg gewöhnt. Vielleicht waren alle unsere Freunde tot.

„Ja, Jupp hat mir auch von Merkse erzählt. Annemie, Marie und Ketta wohnen noch in der alten Wohnung, aber Hella ist jetzt in Frankfurt."

Tante Hella war immer meine Lieblingstante, „Ich kann mich noch erinnern wie Tante Hella vor dem Krieg in der Metzgerei arbeitete. Sie hat mir immer ein dickes Stück Fleischwurst, als wir da einkaufen gingen gegeben.Warum ist sie denn in Frankfurt?" wollte ich wissen. Ich bezeichnete neuerdings alle meine Gedanken mit „vor dem Krieg" oder „nach dem Krieg."

"Frankfurt is a big German city in the American Occupation Zone. The Americans have built a big airport, called Rhein-Main, there. Aunt Hella works in the large American Department Store that has all kinds of things we Germans can't get, such as cigarettes, coffee, chocolate, groceries, and what not all," explained my mother. "Sometimes Aunt Hella can get things that can't be bought in German stores. That's why I would like to go to Frankfurt, too. Perhaps I can do a lot of sewing there and earn enough money to buysome of those things. I'd be able to bring coffee to Oma and I could bring you some chocolate." Suddenly, my mother was all enthused.

The very thought that the terrible poverty of the post-war years might come to an end one day cheered up my mother.

"But Oma and I are going to miss you. I love you so much, Mutti, and I want to go with you," I whined.

"No, child, you have to stay here with Oma. She will take good care of you. When the times are normal again, and the trains are running back and forth regularly, I'll come to get you. Then we can go to Koblenz, or to Frankfurt, or wherever you want to go."

"Yes," I agreed quietly. My mother, my hero! Whenever she made up her mind about something, even the bombs in the war couldn't stop her.

„Frankfurt ist eine grosse deutsche Stadt in der jetzigen amerikanischen Zone. Die Amerikaner haben dort einen grossen Flugplatz, Rhein-Main, gebaut. Tante Hella arbeitet in dem grossen amerikanischen Geschäft. Da können die Amerikaner alles was sie wollen kaufen, wie Zigaretten, Kaffee, Schokolade, Lebensmittel und was nicht alles," erklärte Mutti. „Manchmal bekommt Tante Hella auch solche Sachen die es garnicht in deutschen Geschäften gibt. Deshalb möchte ich auch eventuell nach Frankfurt. Da gibt's bestimmt viel Näharbeit, und ich könnte Geld verdienen. Dann könnte ich der Oma Kaffee und dir Schokolade mitbringen," Mutti war auf einmal ganz begeistert.

Der Gedanke, daß die schreckliche Armut der Nachkriegszeit mal ein Ende findet, machte meine Mutti wieder heiter.

„Oma und ich werden dich aber sehr vermissen. Ich hab' dich doch so gern, Mutti, und will mitgehn," jammerte ich.

„Nein, Kind, du musst hier bei der Oma bleiben. Sie versorgt dich. Wenn die Zeiten wieder normal sind, und die Züge fahren wieder hin und her, hole ich dich ab. Dann fahren wir nach Koblenz, und nach Frankfurt oder wohin du willst."

„Ja," meinte ich ganz leise. Meine Mutter, meine Heldin! Wenn sie sich was in den Kopf setzte, konnten sogar die Bomben sie nicht davon abhalten.

111

Our home in Macken was the old house of my grandmother's family. Her older sister Katt and her husband Nikola had been living there for years. The oldest nephew of Aunt Katt and my Oma had inherited the house, but he didn't require much rent. The house was known to the Mackeners as "the Hospese." The ground floor at the front, where the tavern used to be, was rented to a family that was not related to us.

Our part of the house was at the left side with its own entrance. Aunt Katt and Uncle Nikola occupied the downstairs parlor and one upstairs bedroom. My Oma and Opa had transformed the other upstairs rooms into a comfortable apartment with the furniture they had brought with them from Koblenz. With Oma's pride and joy, the shiny enamel kitchen stove and the familiar cupboard, the kitchen looked very much like the one we had left behind. There was also a sort of loft that had become a living room, but we hardly ever used that space. It was not comfortable because it was usually either too cold or too hot. The house was built very much like the other farm houses in a style called Framework. Even though water lines had been put in, we seldom had running water at the time I lived there. The electric waterpump in the little woods above the village didn't function regularly. The electric wiring had been installed, but the power was very sporadic and undependable. The house had no indoor plumbing, so we had a stinky little outhouse next to the manure pile in the backyard. That's where we could relieve and wipe ourselves with leaves or pages of an old book.

Our kitchen stove was connected to the centrally located chimney with a long black stove pipe.

Ich lernte, dass unser Heim in Macken die alte Heimstätte meiner Oma war. Ihre ältere Schwester Katt und ihr Mann Nikola wohnten schon lange Jahre dort. Der eigentliche Besitzer war ein Neffe von Oma und Katt, aber er forderte nicht viel Miete von der Familie. Die Mackener nannten das Haus „die Hospese." Unten rechts, wo früher die Wirtschaft war, war jetzt eine abgetrennte Wohnung, wo eine fremde Familie wohnte.

Unser Teil des Hauses war auf der linken Seite. Tante Katt mit Onkel Nikola bewohnten ein Zimmer Parterre und ein Schlafzimmer im ersten Stock. Oma und Opa hatten sich oben gemütlich gemacht. Es gab eine Küche mit Omas beliebtem Küchenherd und sonstige Möbel die sie aus Koblenz mitgebracht hatten. Neben Tante Katts Schlafzimmer war unser Schlafzimmer, und da war noch eine große Diele neben der Treppe. Die Diele war als Wohnzimmer eingerichtet, aber da gingen wir fast nie hinein. Es war einfach nicht gemütlich, besonders wenn das Wetter zu kalt oder zu warm war. Das Haus war wie die anderen Bauernhäuser in Macken aus Fachwerk gebaut. Obwohl eineWasserleitung eingebaut war, gab es selten fließendes Wasser zu der Zeit, weil die elektrische Dorfwasserpumpe oben im Wäldchen fast nie funktionierte. Elektrische Leitungen waren auch eingebaut, aber der Strom kam nur sporadisch durch. Das Haus hatte keine eingebaute Toilette, aber wir hatten ein wunderbares Häuslein neben einem Misthaufen im Hof wo man sich erleichtern und mit Laub oder Buchseiten abwischen konnte.

Ein Schornstein, der mitten des Hauses eingebaut war, bediente unseren Küchenherd mit Anschluss durch ein schwarzes Ofenrohr.

"Come along, Marianne, I want to introduce you to some of my friends in the village," Oma challenged me one day.

"Where are we going, Oma?"

"First we're going to Piersche. They are school friends of mine. Piersche Emma and I were in the same class. Piersche Marie and her husband August are also living there. You have to behave yourself and not embarrass me."

"But Oma, I always behave myself!"

Piersche's farmhouse was diagonally across the street. We were always welcome there. Their family name was actually Börsch, but in the local vernacular, their house was called the "Piersche." I was especially interested in the parlor because of the two spinning wheels. When Emma and Marie weren't busy with housework or farm chores, they sat at their spinning wheels turning the raw fleece from sheep into usable yarn. Sometimes they let me help. They didn't let me touch the wheels, but I was allowed to hold up my hands so they could take the spun yarn off the spindle and wind it into skeins.

"Why are we doing this, Aunt Emma?" Nosy me, I wanted to know it all while I held up my hands and let Aunt Emma wind the yarn around my hands.

„Komm mit, Marianne, ich will dich mal im Dorf vorstellen,"
forderte Oma mich eines Tages auf.

„Wohin gehn wir, Oma?"

„Zuerst gehn wir bei Piersche. Das sind Jugendfreunde von
mir. Piersche Emma und ich sind zusammen zur Schule gegangen.
Piersche Marie und ihr Mann August wohnen auch da. Du mußt
aber brav sein und mich nicht blamieren."

„Aber Oma, ich bin doch immer brav!" bestätigte ich.

Piersche hatten ihren kleinen Bauernhof schräg gegenüber
von uns. Wir waren bei ihnen immer willkommen. Ihr
Familienname war eigentlich Börsch, aber im Mackener Platt hieß
das Haus „die Piersche." Die Wohnstube interessierte mich
besonders wegen den beiden Spinnrädern. Emma und Marie, wenn
sie nicht mit Haus- oder Bauernarbeit beschäftigt waren, saßen
immer am Spinnrad. Manchmal durfte ich behilflich sein. Spinnen
ließen sie mich nicht, aber ich durfte die Hände hochhalten und die
gesponnene Schafswolle um meine Hände legen lassen.

„Warum machen wir das, Tante Emma?" wollte ich natürlich
wissen. Brav hielt ich die Hände hoch und ließ Tante Emma die
Wolle um meine Hände wickeln.

I can't leave the wool on the spindles because I have only two. I'll need them for the next batch of wool. The wool also has to be washed again, That's why we wind it into loose skeins. Then we can clean the wool and let it bleach in the sun on a patch of grass." explained Aunt Emma.

"Yes, otherwise the wool would stink like a sheep!" Even Uncle August, who was usually quite serious, laughed at his own joke and my curiosity.

Right next to Piersche, lived the "Kahre" family. Kahre Zillsche (Cecilia) was my mother's favorite friend whenever the Küppers family visited Macken. Zillsche immediately took me into her heart. The Kahre house was directly across the street from ours. They had a little girl about my age named Hiltrud, and we became good friends. It was also in Kahre's front yard where I was first allowed to witness the slaughter of a hog.

The slaughter of the hogs occurred every year in October or November throughout the village. One of the farmers was also a trained butcher. He made the rounds to all the villagers who wanted to slaughter a hog for their winter supply of meat. The horrible screaming of pigs could be heard a couple of times every day. I held my hands over my ears because I didn't want to think about the dying pigs. The work of preparing the sausages, the bacon and cooking the blood soup was done after the hog had been bled properly. All of this activity was highly interesting and exciting for me even though I didn't want to eat most of the products.

„Ich kann die Wolle nicht auf den Spindeln lassen, weil ich die Spindeln für's nächste Mal brauch. Die Wolle muss auch gewaschen werden. Deshalb drehen wir sie in lange Stränge. Dann können wir die Wolle richtig sauber machen und auf der Wiese bleichen lassen." erklärte Tante Emma.

„Ja, sonst stinkt die Wolle ja wie ein Schaf!" Sogar Onkel August, der sonst sehr ernst war, lachte über meine Neugier.

Direkt neben Piersche wohnten die Kahre. Kahre Zillsche war eine Freundin von meiner Mutter. Als Kinder spielten sie zusammen wenn die Küpperse Familie einen Besuch nach Macken machte. Jetzt nahm Zillsche mich sofort in ihr Herz. Kahres Haus und Hof lagen direkt gegenüber wo ich oft mit Hiltrud, eine Nichte von Zillsche, spielte. Im Kahre Hof durfte ich auch zum ersten Mal das Schlachten von einem Schwein beobachten.

Jedes Jahr im Oktober und November wurden im Dorf Schweine geschlachtet. Ein Bauer, der auch gelernter Schlachter und Metzger war, machte die Runde von Hof zu Hof. Da war jeden Tag ein schreckliches Geschrei im Dorf, und ich hielt mir die Ohren zu. Ich wollte nicht an das sterbende Schwein denken. Nachdem ein geschlachtetes Schwein abgeblutet war fing die Arbeit erst richtig an. Es mußte Wurst gemacht, Blutsuppe gekocht und Speck eingesalzen werden. Mir gefiel das Alles als hochinteressante und aufregende Beschäftigung obwohl ich manches davon garnicht essen wollte.

One time I went along with a couple of naughty boys who wanted to play a trick on my aunt Katt. "Don't say anything, Marianne. We're going to wrap this pig's tail in a paper and give it to Aunt Katt as if it were a good sausage. Then we'll run away."

Aunt Katt was thrilled to receive that wrapped "sausage" until she realized the truth. Then she lost her temper and ran after the boys swinging her broom over her head. I laughed like crazy until my Oma caught up with me. She gave me a good whacking on the behind, and then I had to sit in a corner for a while.

"Don't you dare ever laugh at Aunt Katt again! She is my sister, and even if she is old and wrinkled, she does deserve to be ridiculed like that. You'll be old one day. You wouldn't want naughty children to laugh at you, would you?" Oma was very angry. Later I took a bouquet of wildflowers to Aunt Katt and I apologized. She gave me a big hug.

I took Aunt Katt to be a very old woman who couldn't do anything as well as my Oma. Her garden was a pitiful effort next to our lush rows of vegetables and flowers. Not many plants actually grew there, so she depended on the good will of her neighbors who shared produce and milk with her. Oma and Opa generously shared their winter food supply with Aunt Katt and Uncle Nikola.

When we had company, like my mother or Aunt Leni from Berlin, Aunt Katt offered what I hesitate to call her bed.

Einmal lachte ich mit, als ein Paar Buben einen Streich an Tante Katt spielen wollten. „Sag nichts, Marianne. Wir packen den Schweineschwanz in Papier und sagen deiner Tante Katt, Kahre hätten ihr eine gute Wurst gesandt. Dann laufen wir weg."

Tante Katt packte freudenstrahlend die „Wurst" aus. Mit einer Wut erkannte sie sofort den Streich und lief hinter den Jungen mit einem Besen her. Ich lachte mich kaputt bis die Oma mich erwischte. Da bekam ich einen Klops auf den Po und musste eine Weile im Eckchen sitzen.

„Lach mir ja nicht mehr die Tante Katt aus! Das ist meine Schwester und wenn sie noch so alt und verhunzelt ist, hat sie das Auslachen nicht verdient. Du wirst auch mal alt. Du willst doch nicht, daß freche Kinder dich auslachen, oder?" Oma war sehr böse. Nachher brachte ich Tante Katt einen Blumenstrauß und entschuldigte mich. Sie drückte mich fest und gab mir einen Kuss.

Tante Katt war in meinem Begriff schon eine sehr alte Frau die nichts so gut wie meine Oma tun konnte. Ihr Garten war ein erbärmliches Geschöpf neben unserem üppigen. Nicht viel wuchs dort, und sie verließ sich auf gutmütige Nachbarn die ihr frische Bohnen oder andere Gemüse und Milch brachten. Oma und Opa teilten auch grosszügig ihren Wintervorrat mit ihr.

Wenn wir Besuch, wie meine Mutti oder Tante Leni aus Berlin hatten, bot Tante Katt mir ihre Schlafstätte an.

"Oma, do I have to sleep with Aunt Katt?"

"Yes, Marianne, Aunt Katt was kind enough to offer, and you know that her bed is always nice and warm." Oma knew how my night would go, so she laughed at me.

Yes, I knew about Aunt Katt's bed. It was a narrow mountain range of lumpy mattresses, blankets, pillows, and rags of different colors. On cool afternoons she put several bricks and crocks filled with water into the oven. In the evening she wrapped those things in the rags and placed them in her bed. When it was time to go to bed, we had to squirm around the bricks and crocks till we had enough room for our legs and go to sleep.

„Oma muss ich denn wirklich bei Tante Katt schlafen?"

„Ja, Mariannche, die Tante Katt hat es angeboten, und du weißt, daß ihr Bett immer schön warm ist," lachte Oma.

Ja, das wußte ich schon. Ihr Bett war ein Gebirge von unebenen Matratzen, Decken, Kissen und was nicht alles. An kühlen Tagen legte sie schon nachmittags paar Bausteine und mit Wasser gefüllte Krüge in ihren Backofen. Die wurden dann abends in Handtücher eingewickelt und ins Bett gelegt. Wenn wir dann ins Bett gingen mussten wir zuerst mal diese Sachen so umlegen, daß wir für unsere eigene Beine Platz hatten.

The baking days were my favorite. Between the upper village and the lower village was the plaza where three streets came together. The road to Burgen went South. The church was set back to the North, and the Backes was on the other side of the plaza. On Sundays after the Church service, the Mackeners assembled on the plaza to hear the latest news or vote on important local issues. We children were not allowed to stand in the circle of the voting adults. They chased us away when we came too close. On weekdays, the plaza was a more friendly place for the children. Every day someone was baking bread, and it always smelled wonderful.

"Oma, may I help you this time?" I would have loved to learn how to bake bread, but I was still too little, and the ingredients too scarce. We couldn't waste even one drop of milk or one spoon of sugar. Even the flour had to be carefully rationed to last through the winter.

"Child, you have to have strong arms for the kneading. When you are big enough, I'll let you learn, but for now you just get to watch me. If you behave yourself, I'll bake you an apple cookie." Oma always baked an apple cookie out of a bit of dough. Perhaps she learned how to do that from her own mother. She diced a fresh apple into tiny pieces, added a bit of sugar and kneaded them into a ball of dough. Then she banged on the ball with her fist till it looked like a large cookie. That's why I called it my "apple cookie." This cookie was then baked along with the other loaves in the Backes.

Am Liebsten waren mir die Backtage. Zwischen dem Mackener Oberdorf und dem Unterdorf lag ein grosser freier Platz wo die Strassen sich teilten. Die Kirche stand ein bißchen zurückgelegt auf einer Seite, und der Backes war auf der anderen Seite. Sonntags nach der Messe vesammelten sich die Mackener in einem grossen Kreis auf dem Platz und hörten dem Bürgermeister zu. Manchmal mussten die Leute über etwas wählen. Wir Kinder durften nicht im Kreis mitwählen und wurden weggejagt, wenn wir zu nahe kamen. An Werktagen war der Platz mehr kinderfreundlich. Es wurde jeden Tag Brot gebacken, und der Geruch stieg einem angenehm in die Nase.

„Oma, darf ich dir dieses Mal helfen?" Ich hätte so gern das Brotbacken gelernt, aber ich war noch zu klein, und die Zutaten waren zu knapp. Wir durften keinen Tropfen Milch oder Löffel Zucker verschwenden. Mehl mußte auch vorsichtig eingeteilt werden.

„Kind, du mußt starke Armen für das Kneten haben. Wenn du groß genug bist, lasse ich dich lernen, aber jetzt guckst du mir nur zu. Wenn du brav bist, backe ich dir deinen Apfelplatz." Oma hat mir immer einen Apfelplatz aus einem Restchen von dem Brotteig gebacken. Vielleicht hatte sie das von ihrer Mutter gelernt. Sie schnitt einen Apfel in kleine Stückchen, nahm ein bißchen Zucker und knetete sie in einen Ball aus dem Teig. Dann schlug sie mit der Faust auf den Ball bis er wie ein großes Plätzchen aussah. Deshalb habe ich ihn „Platz" gennant.Dann wurde er mit den Broten im Backes gebacken.

Macken had about eighty small farms, and every family had to bake its own bread. That meant that there was a lot of traffic in the Backes. In order to keep some order, the villagers had developed a tradition. The Backes had two large fire chambers. There was room to bake enough bread for a two-week supply, but a baker had to make an appointment to use the ovens. Those who wanted to bake the following day, had to arrive at exactly ten o'clock in the morning to draw lots for their starting time the next day.

"What are they doing with that knife, Oma?"

"First every woman whittles her own design into a piece of wood, called a lot, then she tosses this lot into the apron that one of the women is holding up. A child then draws the lots in order. They've been doing that for hundreds of years. I was also allowed to watch my mother. This time you may draw the lots."

I pulled a piece of wood out of the apron. It didn't belong to my Oma. "You're not first, Oma."

"That's good, because the first one has to bring her dough and wood here very early and start heating up the fire chambers. When I get here as the second or third baker, I won't need so much wood because the ovens are still warm. I still have to start another fire, though; otherwise, the loaves won't bake properly." I loved the way Oma was able to explain things to me. "Marianne, the baking goes on all day. That's why I have to do all the preparing and kneading of the dough at home. Tomorrow we'll bring the dough and the wood here. You'll be able to watch how I use the paddle to move the loaves and your apple cookie into the embers."

Macken hatte ungefähr achtzig Bauernhöfe, und jede Familie backte ihr eigenes Brot. Das heißt, daß viel Betrieb im Backes war. Um Ordnung zu behalten hatten sich die Leute schon eine Tradition angewöhnt. Im Backes waren zwei große Backöfen. Da konnte man genug Brot für zwei Wochen backen, aber man mußte sich schon am Tag vorher anmelden. Punkt zehn Uhr morgens kamen die Frauen die am nächsten Tag Brot backen wollten zum Backes. Dann schnitzten sie ein Stückchen Holz.

„Was machen die mit dem Messer da, Oma?"

„Erst schnitzt jede Frau ein Stückchen Holz, ein Los genannt, mit ihrem eigenen Muster, und dann wirft sie ihr Stückchen Los in eine hochgehaltene Schürze. Das haben die Frauen schon vor Jahrhunderten gemacht. Ich durfte auch meiner Mutter zugucken. Dieses Mal darfst du das Los ziehen."

Ich zog ein Stückchen Holz aus der Schürze. Es gehörte aber nicht der Oma. „Du bist nicht die Erste, Oma."

„Das ist gut, nähmlich die Erste muss schon sehr früh ihren Teig und Holz hierhinbringen, und die Backöfen aufheizen. Wenn ich dann als Zweite nachkomme, brauch ich nicht so viel Holz mitbringen, denn die Backöfen sind noch von der letzten Bäckerin warm. Trotzdem muss ich noch mehr Feuer machen, sonst backen die Brote nicht richtig." Oma konnte mir alles so schön erklären. „Marianne, es wird hier den ganzen Tag gebacken. Deshalb muss ich den Teig daheim ansetzen und kneten. Dann bringen wir den Teig und das Holz morgen hierhin. Du darfst zugucken wie ich die Brote und deinen Apfelplatz auf dem Schieber in die Glut schiebe."

"Bah, Oma, do I have to eat the ashes:"

"No, do you see this rake? When the fire goes out and all the logs are burned up, I'll use the rake to pull out the embers and the ashes. Of course, a little bit of ash always get left behind, but it doesn't hurt anything because the fire cleans everything." Oma was right about that. I had never noticed the bits of ash on the crust of the bread.

"Now we'll go home and start with the sourdough. Tomorrow we'll bake the bread." On the way home, Oma explained how a bit of sourdough is preserved from week to week in a cloth bag hanging near the kitchen stove. Each time new bread is baked a little bit of the dough is crumbled up, put in the bag and saved as leavening for the next batch of fresh bread. Asking many questions, I watched as Oma worked with the dough and baked the bread.

"Now watch out, that you don't burn your fingers and your mouth. You should wait a while with your apple cookie, Marianne." I was standing expectantly right next to Oma as she used a wooden paddle to pull my cookie out of the hot fire chamber.

"But Oma, it smells so good. I can hardly wait," I whined. Soon she pulled out the beautifully browned loaves of bread. Then we had to make room for the next baker.

Every other week, Oma and I almost made a party out of the baking day. Sometimes she told me about her grandmother and her mother as they carried out the same traditions of baking their own bread.

„Bah, Oma, muss ich denn die Asche essen?"

„Nein, siehst Du diesen Schieber? Wenn das Feuer ausgeht nehme ich den Rechenschieber und ziehe die Asche raus, aber da bleibt immer ein bißchen Asche im Ofen. Es schadet nichts, weil Feuer alles sauber macht." Oma hat wieder Recht gehabt. Man konnte das bißchen Asche am Brot garnicht schmecken.

„Wir gehn jetzt heim und setzen den Teig mit dem Sauerteig an. Morgen backen wir." Auf dem Heimweg erzählte Oma mir von dem Sauerteig in dem Stoffbeutel neben dem Küchenherd. Der Sauerteig wurde zum neuen Teig gebraucht. Ein kleines Restchen von dem Teig würde dann in dem Beutel bis zum nächsten Backtag trocknen und für einen neuen Teig verwendet. Ich guckte neugierig zu wie Oma mit der Brottruhe und dem Teig fertig wurde.

„Jetzt pass auf, daß du dir die Finger und den Mund nicht verbrennst. Du kannst doch noch ein Weilchen mit dem Apfelplatz warten, Marianne." Ich stand begeistert direkt neben Oma, als sie meinen Apfelplatz mit dem Schieber aus dem Backofen zog.

„Aber Oma, er riecht so gut! Ich kann kaum warten," jammerte ich. Die Brote kamen zunächst heraus. Dann mussten wir Platz für die nächste Bäckerin machen.

Alle zwei Wochen machten Oma und ich fast eine Feier aus dem Backtag. Manchmal erzählte sie von ihrer Grossmutter Maria, und ihrer Mutter, Barbara, die auch im selben Backes ihr Brot gebacken hatten.

"Oma, you know something? I would love to go to school. Isn't there any school in Macken?" I started a whole new conversation.

"Oh sure, we have a school, but during the war we didn't have any teachers. Anyway, now it's summer vacation, but we're supposed to get a new teacher in September. Mr. Zensen is known to be a good teacher from a city. His wife is very sick. That's why he wants to work in a country village with fresh air and plenty of food. Then you can start going to school in September. You already know how to read, and you've learned some math from your Mutti and your Opa. I'm sure you'll do well in your classes."

"Yes, I can read, but my writing is awful," I was worried and started complaining.

"We'll buy you a school slate and a few styluses, Then you can practice with Opa." Oma always knew how to calm me down.

A few months later I wasn't so enthused about my writing anymore. The hard slate styluses made a screeching noise against the slate, and the little wet sponge smelled yucky in its little tin can. I had a hard school bag that hung awkwardly on my back and shifted back and forth. The whole idea of school had become a lot less appealing than I expected. Mr. Zensen and Pastor Andreas were somehow able to make learning fun despite all the inconveniences. Gradually, I began to feel comfortable and even made a few special friends among my classmates.

„Oma, weißt Du was? Ich würde so gerne in die Schule gehn. Gibt's denn keine Schule in Macken?" fing ich eines Tages an.

„Doch, wir haben eine Schule, aber wir hatten im Krieg keinen Lehrer. Jetzt sind sowieso die Sommerferien. Im September werden wir einen neuen Lehrer bekommen.Der Herr Zensen soll ein guter Lehrer aus einer Stadt sein. Seine Frau ist sehr krank. Deshalb will er jetzt auf einem Dorf, wo frische Luft und genug zu Essen gibt, arbeiten. Dann kannst du im September mit der Schule anfangen. Du hast ja schon gut Lesen und Rechnen von deiner Mutti und dem Opa gelernt und wirst bestimmt nicht sitzenbleiben."

„Ja, ich kann lesen, aber mein Schreiben ist doch furchtbar." meinte ich.

„Wir kaufen Dir eine Tafel und paar Griffel. Dann kannst du mit Opa üben." Oma wußte immer wie man mich beruhigen konnte.

Paar Monate später war ich nicht mehr so von dem Schreiben begeistert. Die Griffel machten komische Geräusche auf der Tafel, und der kleine nasse Schwamm roch ekelhaft in seiner Büchse. Ich hatte einen schwarzen Ranzen der sehr steif auf meinem Rücken hin- und herwackelte. Die ganze Schulsache hatte sich wesentlich meiner Meinung nach verschlimmert. Herr Zensen und der Pfarrer Andreas konnten aber das Lernen trotz den Unbequemlichkeiten interessant machen. Langsam lebte ich mich ein und spielte auch mit meinen Mitschülern.

For fun, we children spent a lot of time in the "Wällsche." This was a small forest of about 10,000 square yards located right next to the school. We could run around among the trees without danger. In the fall, we found blueberries growing on the forest floor. On one side, close to the main road, the village water pump was housed in a small brick building. From one side we could easily climb on the roof of that building and scream into a ventilator pipe on the top. A spooky voice echoed back to give us goosebumps. Then we entertained each other with ghost stories until we got scared enough to run away.

We children were not allowed to go into the other forests surrounding the village without adult supervision. They were afraid we might get confused and not find the way home.

Oma and Opa often took me along when they went to gather wood or edibles. Opa knew about mushrooms, and we especially looked for chanterelles for one of Oma's favorite sauce recipes. When we had chanterelles and boiled potatoes, I didn't need anything else to be satisfied. We also found other things in the forest, such as hazelnuts, raspberries, wild strawberries and especially beechnuts.

"Oma, what are we going to do with all these little beechnuts? They're so small and hard that my fingers hurt when I try to open them. I'd rather eat hazelnuts or walnuts.!"

Zum Zeitvertreib verbrachten wir Kinder viel Zeit im „Wällsche." Ein kleiner Wald (oder Wäldchen) von etwa 10.000 Quadratmeter wuchs unmittelbar neben der Schule. Da konnte man ohne Gefahr herumrennen und Blaubeeren auf der Walderde pflücken. Entlang der Landstrasse im Wällsche, stand die Wasserpumpe des Dorfes. Die Pumpe war in ein kleines Gebäude eingehüllt. Von einer Seite konnten wir ganz leicht auf das Dach klettern und in ein Ventilrohr schreien. Das hat immer so ein unheimliches Echo zurückgeschallt. Dann haben wir uns gegenseitig mit Gespenstergeschichten Angst gemacht und sind schnell wieder weggelaufen.

In andere Wälder durften wir Kinder nicht ohne erwachsene Begleitung gehen. Da könnte man sich verlaufen und den Heimweg nicht mehr finden.

Oma und Opa nahmen mich oft in diese Wälder mit. Opa suchte dort Pilze, besonders Pfifferlinge, die Oma in ein wunderbares Gericht verwandelte. Wenn's Pfifferlinge mit Omas leckere Soße auf Kartoffeln gab, brauchte ich sonst nichts, um mich satt zu essen. Wir ernteten auch andere Naturfrüchte, so wie Haselnüsse, Himbeeren, wilde Erdbeeren, und besonders Bucheckern.

„Oma, was machen wir denn mit den kleinen Bucheckern? Die sind auch so klein und hart, daß mir die Finger weh tun wenn ich sie aufmachen will. Ich esse lieber Haselnüsse oder Walnüsse!"

"Child, beechnuts are not for eating raw," explained Oma. "We collect them because we can have them pressed into a wonderful oil in the oil mill in Burgen. You'll see how we're going to do this. Opa made a huge sieve so that we can separate the little beechnuts from the leaves and other debris. Now watch!"

I watched enthusiastically as Oma dumped a big shovelful of stuff off the forest floor into Opa's sieve. Opa then shook the sieve with his strong arms. The little beechnuts fell through the sieve into a basket. Then Opa poured the beechnuts into a burlap sack. We kept up this routine until we had several sacks full. Then we dragged them home on the cart Opa had built just for this purpose. At home the rest of our work would start right after dinner.

Beechnuts are tiny triangular nuts in a hard outer shell that had to be removed. Each triangle was covered with a thin hard shell that could be left on. Oma' had a method of removing the outer shell that didn't involve breaking our fingernails.

First she spread the nuts on a baking sheet and placed it in the oven for a few minutes. We had to be careful not to burn them but only warm them enough so they could be pried open with a knife. After a few hours of this painstaking work, we put the clean and sorted beechnuts back into a clean sack. The next day we dragged our treasure to the oil mill in Burgen. In exchange for each sack of beechnuts, we received one liter bottle of beechnut oil. As compensation for his work, the miller kept the residue of the

„Kind, Bucheckern sind nicht zum Essen," erklärte Oma. „Wir sammeln sie, weil man daraus wunderbares Öl in der Ölmühle in Burgen pressen lassen kann. Du wirst schon sehn wie wir das machen. Opa hat ein großes Sieb aus Draht gemacht, damit wir zuerst die kleinen Bucheckern von dem Laub trennen. Jetzt pass auf!"

Ich guckte begeistert zu, als Oma eine Schaufel voller Laub und anderem Kram von der Walderde in das Sieb schüttetete. Opa schüttelte kräftig bis unten die Bucheckern in einen Korb fielen. Nachher schüttetete Opa den Korb in einen Zentnersack aus. Das ging so weiter bis wir zwei oder drei Säcke voll hatten. Dann schleppten wir alles auf einer Schubkarre die Opa selbst gebaut hatte wieder nach Hause, wo die Arbeit erst richtig anfing.

Bucheckern sind kleine harte dreieckige Nüsse mit sharfen Kanten in einer runden harten Hülle. Die mussten geschält in die Ölmühle geliefert werden. Oma hatte eine Methode um diese Arbeit zu erleichtern erfunden.

Zuerst legte sie die Bucheckern auf ein Backblech und backte sie paar Minuten im Küchenherd. Man musste aber vorsichtig sein, daß die Bucheckern nicht verbrannten, sondern nur warm genug wurden damit sie mit einem Messer aufgemacht werden konnten. Nach paar Stunden dieser mühsamen Arbeit kamen die sauberen Bucheckern in einen Zentnersack. Am folgenden Tag schleppten wir dann unseren schwererworbenen Schatz in die Ölmühle in Burgen. Man bekam eine Literflasche Öl pro Zentner Bucheckern. Als Lohn

beechnuts. This residue was processed into large bricks that were then sold as feed, fuel or fertilizer. This barter system worked well at a time when natural resources had more value than money.

Beechnut oil is especially delicious for fried or baked goods. I loved the delicate flavor of a piece of my Oma's bread fried in a bit of this precious liquid.

The oil mill in Burgen became an especially favored place for me. The wife of the miller somehow got wind of my mother's sewing talents. This rich lady wanted to hire my mother to refresh her wardrobe. "You can bring Marianne along, Mrs. Simon. We'll entertain her while you're at the sewing machine."

"Mutti, it would be so interesting to watch how they make oil out of those beechnuts! Please, pretty please, let me come with you. I'll be a good girl! Last time when I went with Oma and Opa, I saw a big water wheel on the outside of the building. Part of it was in the creek, so it turned and turned. Opa told me that the energy from this turning wheel made the other machines inside the building work.. But I wasn't allowed to go inside to see those machines."

"Marianne, don't talk so much and don't embarrass me there," Mutti warned me. "In such a mill there are many dangerous machines, and you must listen and obey when the miller tells you something. Perhaps they will let you watch."

für seine Arbeit durfte der Besitzer der Ölmühle den soliden Rest behalten. Es wurde in brauchbare Briketten gepresst und als Brennmaterial, Futter oder Düngermittel verwendet.

Bucheckernöl ist besonders zum Braten lecker. Oma und ich konnten oft den zarten Geschmack von einem Stück Bauernbrot gebraten in Bucheckernöl genießen.

Die Ölmühle wurde mir ein besonders beliebter Platz. Die Frau von dem Ölmüller ertappte, daß Mutti eine gute Schneiderin war und wollte unbedingt ihre Garderobe erneuern. „Bringen Sie ruhig Marianne mit, Frau Simon. Wir werden die Kleine schon unterhalten wenn Sie an der Nähmaschine sitzen."

„Mutti, das wär' doch so interessant zu sehen, wie man Öl aus Bucheckern macht! Bitte, bitte laß mich mitgehn. Ich werde brav sein! Als ich mit Oma und Opa Bucheckern dahin gebracht habe, habe ich ein großes Mühlenrad am Bach gesehn. Opa hat mir erzählt wie die Kraft von dem Mühlenrad die anderen Maschinen treibt. Ich durfte mir aber nicht die Maschinen ansehn. Das wäre doch so interessant, Mutti!"

„Marianne, schwätz nicht so viel und blamiere mich nicht," mahnte Mutti mich. „In so einer Mühle gibt's viele gefährliche Maschinen, und du musst sehr vorsichtig sein und gehorchen, wenn wir da sind. Vielleicht lassen die Leute dich zugucken."

Mutti was invited to work there several times, and she took me along. Her reputation as a good seamstress was well known in Burgen. Not far from the oil mill was a mill for wheat flour where Mutti was also invited to work sometimes. Whenever I went with Mutti, I learned all kinds of things and enjoyed the good food that her grateful clients served.

For a short period of time I lived in Burgen with Mutti. She had decided to settle down in an apartment in Burgen; however, she soon became restless and went back to Frankfurt where she found work with her friend Hella. I was taken back to Macken. In the nine years of my life, I had never lived very long in one place, so it was not difficult for me to get shuffled back and forth. Yet, I felt most comfortable with Oma and Opa in Macken. I could play for hours and hours in peace and quiet. I had time to learn and practice knitting, and I was allowed to read as much as I wanted. Despite my deep love for her, my mother was too restless for me. Although I learned exciting things, whenever I was with my mother, I was always somehow under stress.

Mutti wurde mehrermals dort angestellt. Ihre Schneiderarbeit machte ihr in Burgen einen guten Ruhm. Auch in der Weizenmühle die nicht weit enfernt von der Ölmühle stand, wurde sie zum Schneidern eingeladen.

Eine Zeitlang wohnte ich mit Mutti in Burgen. Sie ließ sich in einer Wohnung nieder, aber sie war nicht lange dort zufrieden und fuhr wieder nach Frankfurt, wo sie bei ihrer Freundin Hella Arbeit fand. Ich wurde wieder in Macken einquartiert. In den neun Jahren meines Lebens hatte ich noch nie lange auf einer Stelle gewohnt, und deshalb fiel mir das Hin-und Herziehen garnicht schwer. Trotzdem fühlte ich mich immer am Wohlsten mit Oma und Opa in Macken. Dort konnte ich in aller Ruhe stundenlang spielen. Ich hatte Zeit zum Strickenlernen- und üben, und durfte lesen so lange ich wollte. Mit Mutti war ich trotz meiner grossen Liebe zu ihr immer irgendwie aufgetrieben und unruhig.

In Macken I found the quietude of nature. The social life of the people depended on the seasonal changes of the harvest. In the spring, the fields had to be plowed and sowed. Gardens were replanted, and calves, lambs, piglets, chicks and other animals were born. In the summer the farm work didn't stop till sundown. Cows had to be milked, the fields worked and winter food supply preserved. Summer was also a time to clean and reorganize. In the fall, the harvest and the butchering began in ernest. In the winter, man and nature rested.

"Marianne, today we're going to harvest peas on our leased field," announced Oma one morning.

"What is a leased field, Oma?"

"Most of the farmers own their fields, but we don't own any. The fields are usually inherited from one generation to another. Because we don't own any fields, we lease, that is like rent, a few of the fields that belong to the community or the parish. We also rent a large walnut tree and four apple trees. We have to pay money to the community every year. Whatever we plant and harvest, we get to keep without having to pay for it in a store. We have one field with peas and one with cabbes..."

I interrupted her again, "Oma, what is cabbes?"

"Oh, I forgot to tell you. Cabbes is cabbage in city language. Out of cabbes we can make sauerkraut. Now let me finish my story. We also have two fields for potatoes and one field for turnips. remember? You like the rübenkraut (thick dark syrup) I make out of the turnips."

In Macken herrschte die Ruhe der Natur. Das Menschenleben richtete sich nach den Jahreszeiten und das Wachsen der Ernte. Im Frühling wurden die Felder gepflügt und gesät. Die Gärten wurden angelegt, und neue Kälber, Lämmer und Küken kamen auf die Welt. Im Sommer hörte die Bauernarbeit nicht bis zum späten Abend auf. Die Kühe mussten gemelkt, die Felder bewacht, die Früchte eingemacht, und die Bauernhöfe geputzt werden. Im Herbst kamen die Ernten und das Schlachten. Im Winter ruhten sich die Felder und die Menschen aus.

„Marianne, heute ernten wir unsere Erbsen auf unserem gepachteten Feld," kündigte Oma eines morgens an.

„Was ist ein gepachtetes Feld, Oma?"

„Die meisten Bauern haben ihre eigenen Felder, Marianne, aber wir besitzen keine. Weil wir aber auch essbare Sachen ernten wollen, können wir paar Felder von der Gemeinde Macken durch den Bürgermeister pachten. Wir haben auch einen großen Nußbaum und vier Apfelbäume gepachtet. Dafür müssen wir der Gemeinde Geld bezahlen. Wenn alles gut wächst, behalten wir unsere Ernte und brauchen diese Lebensmittel nicht kaufen. Wir gehen mit der Schubkarre und ernten unsere eigenen Sachen. Wir haben ein Feld mit Erbsen, ein Feld mit Kabbes..."

„Oma, was ist Kabbes?" fiel ich ihr wieder neugierig ins Wort.

„Ach ja, Kabbes heißt Kohl auf hochdeutsch. Daraus machen wir Sauerkraut. Jetzt laß mich doch fertig reden. Wir haben auch zwei Felder für Kartoffel, und ein Feld für Rüben. Du ißt doch so gern Rübenkraut auf einem Stück Brot, Marianne."

"Yummy, rübenkraut is especially good on buttered bread, but it is always so sticky," I laughed.

"Now we're going to make our sandwiches, and we'll also take some raspberry juice with us. We have a lot of work to do today and probably won't get home till this evening."

Work in the fields was always a lot of fun for us children, no matter whether the adults were picking peas, cutting hay, or harvesting wheat. The grain harvest was especially exciting. After a farmer cut the stalks with a scythe, his wife bound them into bundles which were then stacked for drying. We children ran around the stacks to play hide and seek. A few days later those stacks were carted back to the farm on wagons pulled by cows. Sometimes a farmer let me and a friend ride home on a wagon piled high with wheat or rye.

If we happened to hit a rut in the road, the whole wagon would shake dangerously, threatening us children with injury unless we held tightly to the ropes. Fear mixed with excitement until we finally reached the village with sweaty faces.

After dinner I was usually allowed to go play outside until it got dark. Throughout the village we could hear the farmers hammering their scythes to sharpen them for the next day's cutting. Mixed with the rhythmic hammering, we could also hear the chickens cackling, cows mooing and children screaming at play. Then Opa opened a window and played his concertina. Strains of familiar folksongs told us that all was well with the world. Nothing could match the peaceful summer evenings in Macken.

„Mmm. Rübenkraut. Das schmeckt lecker, aber es ist immer so klebrig!" lachte ich.

„Jetzt machen wir unsere Butterbrote und holen auch Himbeersaft mit, denn wir haben viel Arbeit auf dem Feld und kommen bis heute Abend nicht heim."

Feldarbeit war immer viel Spaß, egal ob die Ernte Erbsen, Heu oder Getreide war. Es waren andere Bauern mit ihren Kindern auf den verschiedenen Feldern. Das Getreide wurde mit einer Sense gemäht und in Garben gebunden. Dann stapelte man die Garben in Kasten auf. Da konnten wir Kinder so schön Versteck hinter den Kasten spielen. Paar Tage später wurden die Getreidegarben auf einem von zwei Kühen gezogenen Wagen heimgebracht. Auf dem Heimweg durfte ich manchmal mit einer Freundin auf einem hochgestapeltem Wagen mitfahren.

Als wir über die unebene Wege rumpelten, wackelte der ganze Wagen und drohte uns Kinder mit Verletzung, wenn wir uns nicht festhielten. Angst mischte sich mit Reizung, und wir kamen endlich wunderbar aufgeregt im Dorf an.

Nach dem Essen durfte ich noch bis es dunkel wurde draussen spielen. Dann konnte man im ganzen Dorf die Hammerschläge des Sensenschärfen hören. Gemischt mit dem Klopfen, dem Gackern der Hühner, und dem Schreien der spielenden Kinder waren die Töne einer Ziehharmonika. Opa saß am offenen Fenster in der Dämmerung und spielte „Waldeslust," „Guter Mond Du Gehst so Stille," oder „Ach, Du Lieber Augustin." Es konnte nichts gemütlicher sein, als diese Sommerabende in Macken.

Unfortunately, Opa could also make life uncomfortable for Oma and me. In the fall, Opa gathered the rotting fruit that had fallen from the trees and put it into two large earthenware crocks. He mixed this rotting fruit with some sugar and yeast to help it ferment. In the backyard next to the manure pile we had two stalls. One was rented to a neighbor to keep his pigs. Opa used the other stall as storage for his precious crocks full of the rotting fruit. The stink of the manure pile covered the foul odor of the fermenting.

"Now don't make such a disgusting mess on my clean kitchen stove!" Oma yelled whenever Opa showed up with his copper tubes. Uncle Nikola followed him with a large kettle.

Opa got loud in advance, "How else am I supposed to brew my schnaps?" Then the bickering between Oma and Opa got started for real. I was used to their game, so I simply ignored them and got interested in the miracle that was developing on the stove.

Opa poured a large portion of the fermented fruit into the kettle. He had heated up the stove, so the stinky mess soon began to boil. The two men watched carefully as the alcohol steam trickled drop by drop through the tubes attached to the tight lid. They caught the precious liquid in a bottle. Opa noticed my fascination, so he said, "You can catch a drop on your fingertip and take a taste."

Uncle Nikola teased me with a mischievous smile, "Come on, Marianne, taste it."

"Ouch, ouch!" I screamed as I felt the raw schnaps on my tongue. I thought it was burning a hole through my tongue.

Leider konnte Opa genau so gut ungemütlich werden. Im Herbst sammelte Opa die Fallfrüchte unter den Bäumen und ließ sie mit irgendwelchen Zutaten wie Zucker und Hefe in zwei riesengroßen Steinkrügen gären. Wir hatten hintem im Hof neben dem Misthaufen zwei Ställe und unser Abhäuschen. Wir hielten selbst kein Vieh außer ein paar Hühner, aber ein Stall war vermietet und brachte zwei Schweine unter. Also stand ein Stall leer. Opa brachte da seine wertvolle Steinkrüge unter. Wegen dem Misthaufen konnte man den Gestank der gärenden Frucht garnicht riechen.

„Jetzt mach mir nicht wieder so'n Mist auf dem Küchenherd!" beschwerte Oma sich jedesmal wenn Opa seine Kupferröhre in die Küche schleppte. Onkel Nikola brachte einen großen Kessel nach.

„Wie soll ich denn sonst meinen Schnaps brauen?" erwiderte Opa und wurde schon im Voraus laut. Dann fing die gewöhnliche Meckerei zwischen Oma und Opa an. Mir, aber, gefiel das Wunder was sich auf dem Herd entwickelte, als ich die beiden Zänker nicht beachtete.

In einem großen Kessel wurde die gegärte Frucht gekocht, bis es so weit war, daß der Dunst nach oben stieg. Ein Deckel mit den angehefteten Kupferröhren fing den Dunst und ließ ihn durch die lange Kupferschlinge in eine Flasche tröpfen. Einmal durfte ich so einen Tropfen mit meinem Finger fangen.

„Marianne, versuch doch mal wie so was schmeckt," lockte Onkel Nikola mich.

„Ou-ah!" schrie ich, als ich den Tropfen auf meiner Zunge spürte. Ich dachte es würde mir ein Loch in die Zunge brennen.

Both men laughed at me, so I got mad.

"Here, drink a bit of this raspberry juice, and take a lesson from this. Don't ever drink any alcohol, Marianne." Opa said, but sadly, he didn't take his own advice. After the brewing of a bottle of schnaps, we always had a few days of turmoil. Oma and Opa had big fights about his drinking. Sometimes we had to spend the night at Piersche's because of Opa's roaring and loud snoring,

Despite his violent temper toward my Oma, Opa always treated me with love and tenderness. He played cards with me and told me tall tales. He taught me songs, and accompanied them on his concertina. He even let me watch him work in his workshop as much as I wanted. Opa had managed to rescue some of his tools from before the war and brought them to Macken, so he created a workshop in a loft of the barn that was only accessible from the other side of the house. This loft above the stalls was no longer in use for hay storage by the renters of the front apartment, so Opa claimed it for himself.

He had to find a way to climb up there from our side and arrange his workspace. Somehow he built a ladder out of wood he had gathered in the forest. This homemade ladder was simply leaned against the wall toward the opening. I was always a bit scared to climb that ladder with him up to his miraculous laboratory. I was not allowed to touch anything except the rabbits he was raising up there, but I was satisfied just to watch him work. He made good use of a large round grindstone, probably a leftover from the forge, in the yard. He explained everything to me.

Die zwei Männer lachten mich aus.

„Hier, trink ein bißchen Himbeersaft, und laß das eine Lehre sein. Trinke keinen Alkohol, Marianne." Opa kam mir zur Hilfe. Leider nahm er seinen guten Rat nicht selbst an. Nach dem Brauen einer Flasche Schnaps kamen immer paar Tage Unruhe. Oma und Opa hatten dann Streit. Manchmal übernachteten Oma und ich sogar bei Piersche wegen Opas lautem Brüllen und Schnarchen.

Trotzt seiner üblen Laune gegenüber Oma, behandelte Opa mich immer mit Zärtlichkeit und Liebe. Er spielte Karten mit mir, besonders `Bauernlegen.' Er erzählte mir tolle Geschichten, und sang Lieder die er mit seiner Ziehharmonika begleitete. Ich durfte sogar in seiner Werkstätte so oft zugucken wie ich wollte. Über den Ställen im Hof und der Scheune die nur von der anderen Seite des Hauses zugänglich war, gab es einen Dachboden wo früher Heu und Stroh gespeichert wurde. Jetzt aber wohnten die anderen Mieter und wir in dem Haus ohne richtige Bauernarbeit zu führen. Also stand der Dachboden leer. Opa, der immer sehr geschickt im Handwerk war, zog sich diesen Dachboden als seine eigene Werkstätte zu.

Zuerst musste er sich Zutritt auf unserer Seite des Hauses versorgen. Opa hatte einiges Werkzeug aus dem Krieg gerettet und nach Macken mitgebracht. Irgendwie baute er eine Leiter aus Holz das er selbst im Wald fand. Diese Leiter wurde einfach an die Wand die oben eine Öffnung zur Werkstätte hatte gelehnt. Da kletterten wir Beide vorsichtig herauf um Opas wunderbares Labor zu betreten. Ich durfte nichts außer den Kanienchen, die er dort züchtete berühren. Aber das Zugucken genügte mir. Opa erklärte mir auch immer alles so schön.

"Watch this, Marianne. I'm going to light my pipe with my glasses!"

"Opa, you can't do that. You have to have fire to light your pipe," I argued.

Opa laughed, "Just watch, little Marianne. I'm holding the pipe with fresh tobacco in my left hand and my glasses in my right hand. Then I hold both hands in the sunshine coming through the window. The lens in the glasses collects the rays and concentrates them into one sharp ray that I can aim at the tobacco. Look! It's starting to smoke a little. There! A spark just started the burning. Now I can smoke my pipe."

I was astounded. My Opa was a genius! He even created toys for me. All my dolls of various sizes had their own chairs that he created out of bits of wood and wire. He built stilts for my girlfriend Hiltrud and me. A few weeks later most of the children in the village were wandering around on their "Küpperse" stilts. For the girls he gladly made doll chairs, and for the boys he created locomotives out of trimmed branches. Creating toys gave him the pleasure of making children happy between his more serious jobs as handiman.

Usually he was kept very busy with repair work for the farmers in exchange for food stuff. If a metal milk bucket sprang a leak, Opa's soldering iron took care of the problem in exchange for a few eggs. In case someone wanted to built a new barn, Opa arrived to help with his tools in exchange for a rasher of bacon. As long as he didn't lose his senses from drinking too much schnaps, he was the official repairman of the village.

„Pass mal auf, Marianne. Ich zünde jetzt meine Pfeife mit meiner Brille an!"

„Opa, datt kannste doch net. Dau muß doch Feuer hann." weigerte ich mich. Ich hatte Mackener Platt gelernt.

Opa lachte, „Pass auf, Mariannchen. Ich hole die Pfeife mit frischem Tabak in die linke Hand und meine Brille in die Rechte. Dann halte ich beide Hände in die Sonnenstrahlen die durch das Fenster kommen. Die Linse in der Brille nimmt die Sonnenstrahlen auf und sammelt sie in einen scharfen Strahl, den ich auf den Tabak strahlen lasse. Siehste, jetzt fängt es schon an zu qualmen. Da! Jetzt hat der Tabak den Funk gefangen."

Ich konnte nur staunen. Mein Opa war ein Genie! Alle meine Puppen in jeder Größe hatten ihre eigenen Stühle die er aus Holz und Draht bastelte. Für die Mädchen baute er Puppenstühlchen und für die Jungens wurden Eisenbähnchen aus dünnen Baumstämmen gebaut. Opa machte Stilzen für mich und meine Freundin Hiltrud. Paar Wochen später wanderten die meisten Kinder im Dorf mit ihren „Küpperse" Stilzen herum. Die Spielsachen waren für Opa nur Zwischenarbeit.

Meistens war er sehr mit wichtigerem Flicken für die Bauern gegen Lebensmittel beschäftigt. Kam jemand mit einem Loch im Milcheimer, nahm Opa den Lötkolben und flickte den Eimer im Austausch für paar Eier. Wollte jemand eine neue Scheune bauen, kam Opa mit seinem Werkzeug und half im Austausch für ein dickes Stück Speck. So lange Opa mit seinem Schnaps den Verstand nicht verlor, war er der tüchtige Handwerkmeister des Dorfes.

One day I asked, "Oma, where did Opa learn all these things? He knows how to do things that other men don't know how to do."

"Opa used to be a railroad engineer when he was young. He was retired before the war...." Oma wanted to continue her explanation, but I interrupted her.

"Oma, what is retired?"

"You really are too inquisitive, Marianne. Now listen carefully, so you will learn something." Oma warned me with only a half-angry glance.

"When we got married, Opa worked on the railroad. Then World War I started, and Opa had to become a soldier. At that time we had only two children: Leni, your aunt who lives in Berlin now, and Tilli, your mother, were my little girls. After the war, Opa came home and went back to his job on the railroad, but he started to become a very heavy drinker. We had a lot of fights, but when he wasn't drunk he was a good man."

"He is still a good man, Oma," I said.

"Yes, he is, Marianne, but there were times when he was not."

"Why not, Oma?"

"His drinking got worse and worse. One day he came home and simply said, 'I got fired.' Then I started yelling at him. 'How am I supposed to feed our children?' He just shook his head and left the apartment," Oma explained.

Eines Tages fragte ich, „Oma wie hat Opa das Alles gelernt? Er kann so Vieles, was andere Männer garnicht können."

„Opa war mal Lokführer bei der Eisenbahn, als er noch jung war. Vor dem Krieg hat er sich pensionieren lassen..." Oma wollte erklären, aber ich fiel ihr wieder ins Wort.

„Oma, was heißt, sich pensionieren lassen?"

„Du bist aber wirklich eine Vorwitznase, Mariannchen. Jetzt hör mal gut zu, dann lernst du etwas," Oma warnte mich mit einem halb bösen Blick.

„Als wir uns verheirateten, arbeitete Opa auf der Eisenbahn. Dann kam der erste Weltkrieg, und Opa wurde Soldat. Deine Tante Leni, die jetzt in Berlin wohnt, und deine Mutti waren meine kleine Kinder damals. Nach dem Krieg kam Opa wieder heim, und arbeitete wieder bei der Eisenbahn, aber er wurde ein schwerer Trinker. Wir hatten oft Streit, aber wenn er nicht betrunken war, war er ein guter Mann."

„Er ist immernoch ein guter Mann, Oma," sagte ich.

„Ja, Mariannchen, aber es gab Zeiten, wo Opa nicht so gut war."

„Warum denn nicht, Oma?"

„Seine Trinkerei ist immer schlimmer geworden. Er verspielte sein Geld, und manchmal verprügelte er mich. Eines Tages kam er Heim und sagte, *Ich bin entlassen worden.* Da brüllte ich ihn an.

"What did you do then, Oma? Where did you get money for your family?"

"Child, I went to the railroad office and talked to Opa's boss. I begged him to remember that Opa was a good soldier and a good railroad engineer. That his drinking had only started after the war, and that just a few months earlier, we had another baby, a little boy, so we had three children to support. Then a miracle happened." Oma smiled at me.

"Then what, Oma?" I was as curious as a cat.

"The boss said that they could give Opa a choice of retiring or getting fired. That would mean that we would get paid in the future for the work he had already done in the past. But this could only happen on the condition that the money would come to me because I was taking care of the children. That's why I get money every month to pay the rent for our house and the lease for our fields." Oma looked at me. "Did you understand, Marianne? Now don't talk about this with Opa. He is still very ashamed about this whole experience."

"Yes, Oma, I understand."

"Now I really have to get ready to do the laundry," Oma abruptly changed the subject.

Laundry day was always a difficult day for Oma. She usually ended up with a headache and a backache.

"Do you want me to help you, Oma?"

Wie soll ich dann die Kinder ernähren? Er schüttelte nur den Kopf und verließ unsere Wohnung," erzählte Oma.

„Was hast du denn da gemacht, Oma? Wo hast du denn Geld her bekommen?"

„Kind, ich bin bei die Eisenbahnbehörde gegangen und habe gebittelt und gebettelt. Ich habe sie daran erinnert, daß er einmal ein guter Soldat und ein guter Eisenbahner war, und daß seine Trinkerei nur nach dem Krieg angefangen hatte. Und daß wir vor Kurzem noch ein Kind, ein kleiner Junge, bekommen hatten. Dann passierte ein Wunder."

„Was denn, Oma?" ich war gespannt wie auf heißen Kohlen.

„Der Chef sagte mir, daß Opa pensioniert anstatt entlassen wird. Das heißt, daß er für seine frühere Arbeit jeden Monat bezahlt wird, aber nur unter der Bedingung, daß das monatliche Geld nur mir als Mutter zukommt, weil wir drei Kinder haben. Deshalb bekomme ich jeden Monat Geld, womit ich die Miete und die Pacht bezahlen kann." Oma guckte mich an. „Hast du das verstanden, Marianne? Jetzt sag aber Opa nichts von unserer Unterhaltung. Er hat sich damals sehr geschämt, und spricht nicht gern über dieses Ergebnis."

„Ja, Oma, ich hab' verstanden."

„Jetzt muß ich mich um meine Wäsche kümmern," damit war Oma mit dem Opathema fertig.

"You can bring the basket of dirty clothes down while I get the tub ready." Oma was talking about the big oval galvanized tub that we also used to take a bath on Saturdays. The old tub had lost one of its handles, and Opa had already soldered the leaks several times.

When I arrived with the laundry basket, Oma was just placing the tub on the bench in the yard. "Marianne, will you go get the scrub brush. I'll go get the board."

"Do you want me to get the soap too, Oma?"

"Yes, last week I got a bar of soap from Kahre. They made a whole batch."

"They made it?"

"Yes, our parish priest is an educated man, and after the war, when people couldn't buy things like soap, he did some studying in his books and found out how to make soap out of the parts of a slaughtered pig that people usually don't use. He taught Kahre how to make soap."

"Soap from a pig? Bah!" I stuck out my tongue.

"See, you always want to know everything and then you make a disgusted face when I tell you," Oma chided me. "Now all we need

Waschtag war immer sehr strapazierend für Oma. Nachher hatte sie meistens Kopfweh und Rückenschmerzen.

„Darf ich dir helfen, Oma?"

„Du kannst den Korb mit der Wäsche runterbringen während ich die Waschbütte hole. Omas Waschbütte war dieselbe alte Zinkwanne, die auch als unsere Badewanne diente. Ein Henkel war schon abgebrochen, und Opa verlötete schon paarmal kleine Löcher.

Als ich mit dem Korb ankan, hatte Oma schon die Bütte auf die Bank im Hof gestellt. „Marianne, geh hol' die Schrubbürste. Ich bringe das Bügelbrett." Ihr Bügelbrett war ganz weiß abgescheuert von dem vielen Waschen.

„Soll ich auch die Seife bringen, Oma?"

„Ja, ich habe ein frisches Stück Seife von Kahre bekommen. Die Kahre haben Seife letzte Woche gemacht."

„Seife gemacht?"

„Ja, unser Pfarrer ist ein schlauer und ausgebildeter Mann. Nach dem Krieg, wenn man nichts mehr kaufen konnte, hat er in seinen Bücher studiert, wie man so Sachen wie Seife aus Schweinefett, das sonst nicht brauchbar ist, machen kann."

„Seife aus Schweinefett? Bah!"

„Sieste, du willst immer alles wissen, und dann machst du eine Fratze wenn ich dir etwas erkläre," schimpfte Oma. „Jetzt

153

is the water." Oma had already been boiling water on the kitchen stove, but she didn't want me to carry the hot kettle.

"Marianne, you go get some cold water from the faucet. The pump has been working lately, so we have running water again. Who knows how long that will last."

Once we got all the stuff together, Oma started her scrubbing. There was no more conversation as she laid out one of Opa's shirts on the frequently scoured board and used her scrub brush with a bit of soap to remove the stains.

At the back of our vegetable garden, we had a small lawn where Oma spread the washed whites, such as towels or bedsheets.

"Why are you putting the clean laundry on the ground, Oma?"

"When the sun shines on the white material, it helps to bleach out the germs and makes the things nice and white while they're drying. If the sun keeps shining, I'll take this watering can and wet the white things down one more time. Then I'll hang them up on this line here to make sure they are really dry before I fold them up. I always keep this lawn very clean, and that's why I won't let you play on it. This is my laundry lawn."

"Oma, I didn't know that the sun could bleach things, but now I understand what Piersche Emma told me about bleaching the wool she was spinning. When you put the wet wool in the sunshine, it gets the germs out and makes it white. Is that right, Oma?"

brauchen wir noch Wasser." Oma hatte schon einen grossen Kessel auf den Küchenherd aufgestellt, aber den durfte ich nicht tragen.

„Marianne, geh hol' kaltes Wasser von dem Kranen. Heute haben wir wieder fließendes Wasser. Wer weiß, wie lange die Dorfwasserpumpe noch funktioniert."

Sobald wir mit allem vorbereitet waren, fing Oma an zu schrubben. Da gab's keine Unterhaltung mehr, als sie fleißig auf dem Brett die Flecken an einem Hemd von Opa schrubbte.

Hinten im Garten hatten wir eine kleine Wiese, wo Oma immer ihre weiße Wäsche zum Bleichen und Trocknen ausbreitete.

„Warum legst du die frischgewaschenen Sachen auf die Wiese, Oma?"

„Wenn die Sonne auf den weißen Stoff scheint, bleicht und desinfiziert sie die nasse Wäsche beim Trocknen. Solange die Sonne noch scheint, tue ich nochmal mit dieser Gießkanne Wasser über die Handtücher und Bettwäsche giessen. Dann werden die Sachen auf diese Leinen aufgehangen bis sie ganz trocken sind. Diese Wiese muss deshalb ganz sauber bleiben, und du darfst nicht darauf spielen. Es ist nur meine Bleichwiese."

„Oma, ich habe nicht gewusst, dass die Sonne etwas bleichen kann, aber jetzt verstehe ich was Piersche Emma mir von dem Bleichen ihrer gesponnenen Wolle erzählte. Wenn man die nasse Wolle in die Sonne legt, wird sie weiß und desinfiziert. Richtig, Oma?"

"Yes, if you ever get a chance to study science in high school, you'll learn all about how this happens."

Yes, my Oma was a brave, intelligent and diligent woman who always thought about her family's welfare.

And that's how my interesting life in Macken went on. Whenever I really needed some solitude I visited the village cemetery. After the horrid noises of the war, I sometimes didn't want to see or hear anything and craved only peace and quiet. I was able to find that in the cemetery. I wandered from grave to grave and read the inscriptions on the grave markers. Then I made up stories about the lives of the people buried there. Sometimes I sang little melodies that popped into my head. This was a healing exercise for me, but my mother couldn't understand that. When she came to visit she wouldn't let me go to the cemetery.

"What are you doing there amongst the dead?" she demanded to know. "Don't transform yourself into such a sad creature. All of a sudden you'll start wearing black dresses and make a sad face like your Grandma Simon!"

"But, Mutti, they were all living people once," I argued. "I like to go there because it is so nice and quiet. There are always beautiful flowers and colorful beetles to admire."

"As long as you don't get all depressed!" she warned me again. "Your Grandma Simon snapped from being so depressed all the time, and now she's dead." My mother didn't like her mother-in-law at all.

„Ja, wenn du mal die Wissenschaft auf der Hochschule studierst, wirst du lernen, wie das geht."

Ja, meine Oma war eine tapfere, schlaue, und fleißige Frau, die immer nur an die Wohlfahrt ihrer Familie dachte.

So ging mein Leben in Macken interessant weiter. Wenn ich mal wirklich meine Ruhe brauchte, besuchte ich den Friedhof. Nach dem vielen Lärm des Krieges, wollte ich manchmal garnichts Anderes sehen und hören wie nur die Stille und Frieden. Auf dem Friedhof war jenes zu finden. Ich wanderte von Grab zu Grab und las die Namen und andere Angaben auf den Grabsteinen. Dann dachte ich mir die Lebensgeschichten der Begrabenen aus. Manchmal sang ich kleine Melodien dazu. Das war für mich eine heilsame Beschäftigung, aber Mutti konnte das nicht verstehen. Wenn sie zu Besuch kam, wollte sie mich nicht auf den Friedhof lassen.

„Was willst du denn da unter den Toten?" forderte sie mich auf. „Mach dich doch nicht so ein trauriges Wesen. Nachher kommst du nur noch mit schwarzen Kleidern und saurem Gesicht wie die Simonse Oma daher!"

„Aber Mutti, das waren doch alle mal lebendige Leute," streitete ich ihr ab. „Ich geh doch nur dahin, weil es so schön still ist. Da gibt es immer schöne Blumen und bunte Käfer zum bewundern."

„So lange Du mir nicht demütig wirst!" mahnte sie mich nochmal. „Deine Simonse Oma ist vor lauter Demut übergeschnappt, und jetzt ist sie auch tot." Mutti konnte ihre Schwiegermutter nie

She had experienced a difficult marriage because of her. "Do you know that your father is back in Koblenz? He was released as a prisoner of war last month."

"Is Vati coming to visit me here in Macken?" I hadn't seen him in a long time, but I didn't really care. He had never been a true family man like my Opa. He visited me in Macken one year later, but he really didn't know how to be a father.

There was always something to interest me in Macken. When I first noticed the large metal milk cans in front of each farmhouse, I asked Oma, "Why do they give their milk away?"

Oma explained, "Even when I was a child, every farmer had to declare how many cows he owned. It was his duty as part of a community. The milk cans belong to the dairy in Kastellaun about ten kilometers from here. The farmers were expected to fill one can with fresh milk for every two cows they owned. Now a truck comes to pick up the cans every other day, but when I was a little girl there were no trucks. An oxcart came to pick up the cans."

"But Oma," I objected. "The milk belongs to the farmers. "Why do they have to give it away?"

"I'm getting to that, Marianne. The farmers are part of a community, like Macken, for example. If Macken needs a road or running water or anything else to connect the farmers to other

leiden. Mutti hatte ein schwieriges Leben und eine schwierige Ehe wegen dieser Frau. „Weißt du, daß dein Vati wieder in Koblenz ist? Er ist aus der Gefangenschaft vor einem Monat zurückgekommen."

„Kommt Vati mich hier in Macken besuchen?" Ich hatte ihn schon lange nicht gesehn, aber es machte mir nichts aus. Er war nie ein richtiger Familienvater wie mein Opa. Er kam erst ein Jahr später auf Besuch, aber leider wußte er wirklich nicht, wie man ein Vater ist.

Es gab immer etwas Interessantes in Macken zu beobachten. Als ich zuerst die grossen Milchkannen vor jedem Bauernhaus bemerkte, wollte ich wissen, „Oma, warum geben die Bauern ihre Milch weg?"

„Selbst als ich noch ein Kind war, mußte jeder Bauer seine Kühe anmelden. Das war die Pflicht als Einwohner einer Gemeinde. Die Milchkannen gehören einer Molkerei in Kastellaun, ungefähr zehn Kilometer von hier. Der Bauer soll dann eine Kanne mit Milch von jeden zwei Kühen abfüllen. Jetzt kommt ein Lastwagen alle zwei Tage die Milch abholen. Als ich aber noch ein Kind war, kam eine Ochsenkarre aus der Molkerei die Milch abholen."

„Aber, Oma," weigerte ich mich. „Die Milch gehört doch den Bauern. Warum müssen sie es weggeben?"

„Ich komme noch daran, Marianne. Alle Bauern sind Einwohner einer Gemeinde, wie zum Beispiel, Macken. Wenn die Gemeinde eine Strasse, eine Wasserleitung, oder irgendeine

159

communities, it has to pay money to get these things. How do you think the farmers in Macken can get the money?"

"I guess they have to sell some of the stuff they grow here," I offered. I was beginning to get lost in thought about money.

"Right. One of the things they grow here is a cow. Every cow is very valuable. It gives milk every day, it grows a calf every year, and besides that, two cows harnessed to a wagon can bring in the harvest from the fields. Even the manure is very useful," laughed Oma. "You've seen and smelled how the farmers pile up bunch of manure in a wagon and take it to their fields, haven't you?"

I wrinkled my nose and nodded, "Uh-Hmm."

"That's called fertilizing the field to make the soil richer for next year's plants."

"Yes, my girlfriend Hiltrud and I had some good laughs about the stinky manure in the fields, but I still don't understand about the milk cans."

"Marianne, everything is connected. The whole community depends on each farmer and each cow, so a long time ago they voted to contribute some of the things they grow to improve the community. A group of communities is called a county. Macken is part of the Kastellaun county. The dairy in Kastellaun collects the fresh milk from the communities. Then they do things with the milk, like take some of the fat off the top to make butter to be sold in the cities. They also keep the milk to sell in the cities. That's how the

andere Verbindung mit anderen Gemeinden haben will, müssen die Bauern das Geld aufbringen. Wie kommen dann die Bauern an Geld?"

„Ich meine, sie müssten ein Teil ihrer Ernte verkaufen," schlug ich vor. Ich verlor mich fast in Gedanken über Geld.

„Genau! Nicht nur die Ernte, sondern auch das Vieh. Aber jede Kuh ist sehr wertvoll. Eine Kuh gibt jeden Tag Milch und jedes Jahr ein Kalb. Außerdem, arbeiten die Kühe auch schwer wenn sie die vollbeladenen Wagen aus den Feldern ziehen. Sogar ihr Mist ist wertvoll," lachte Oma. „Du hast doch schon gesehen und gerochen, als ein Bauer einen Wagen mit Mist beladet und auf ein Feld bringt."

Ich schrumpfte meine Nase und nickte, „Ah hmmm."

„Dann heißt der Mist Dünger, der das Feld fruchtbar machen soll, damit nächstes Jahr wieder die Pflanzen gut wachsen."

„Ja, meine Freundin Hiltrud hat mir schon davon erzählt, aber ich verstehe immer noch nichts von den Milchkannen."

„Marianne es ist alles irgendwie verbunden. Die ganze Gemeinde verlässt sich auf jeden Bauer und jede Kuh. Deshalb haben sie schon vor langer Zeit gewählt, dass jeder Einwohner beitragen soll, damit nicht nur eine Gemeinde sondern auch ein Kreis solcher Gemeinden wachsen kann. Die Gemeinde Macken gehört dem Kreis Kastellaun an. Die Molkerei dort sammelt die Milch von den Gemeinden. Dann wird die Milch bearbeitet, wie die Sahne zum Beispiel, abzuziehen. Die Sahne wird dann zu Butter die man in den Städten verkaufen kann gemacht. Die Molkerei behält auch ein Teil

county can get money to build roads or water lines. Then the dairy sterilizes the cans and take them back to the farmers. That's how it was when I was a little girl."

"Is it different now, Oma?" I had noticed a sad look come over her face.

"Yes, the farmers were happy to make their contributions. If someone wanted to keep some of the fat on top of the milk to make their own butter, nobody punished them. Now, after the war, nobody is allowed to make their own decisions. Somebody comes to count how many cows a farmer has. Then three times a week the farmer has to give the right amount of milk, or they are punished. They might have to pay money, or they might have to give one of their cows or pigs, or something. No one is allowed to cheat because people in the cities don't have enough food..."

"I know Oma," I interrupted her. "Uncle Jupp told me about that. People are begging for food in the villages because there aren't any stores in the city."

"Yes, during the war most of the buildings were destroyed in all the cities, not only Koblenz. Even the stores that weren't destroyed can't get their food supplies like before the war, so things got very bad. That's one of the reasons Opa and I moved here to Macken."

"I'm glad, Oma. I like it here."

The connection between Macken and the outside world was made a little clearer, but I didn't really want to think about the things that were happening in the cities.

162

der Milch zum verkaufen. So macht der Kreis Geld um Strassen und andere Verbindungen zu bauen. Die Kannen werden dann an die Bauern zurückgebracht. So war es, als ich ein kleines Mädchen war."

„Ist es denn jetzt anders?" Ich merkte Omas traurige Augen.

„Ja, damals waren die Bauern froh, ihre Beiträge freiwillig zu geben. Wenn jemand mal etwas von der Sahne selbst behalten wollte um Butter zu machen, wurden sie nicht bestraft. Aber jetzt nach dem Krieg darf niemand sich weigern. Jemand von der Behörde kommt die Kühe zählen. Dreimal in der Woche muss der Bauer dann die bestimmten Kannen Milch abliefern, oder er wird bestraft. Zur Strafe könnte er eine Kuh oder ein Schwein verlieren. Keiner darf sich weigern, weil die Leute in den Städten nich genug zu Essen haben..."

„Ich weiß Oma," fiel ich ihr ins Wort. „Onkel Jupp hat mir davon erzählt. Manche Leute gehen in den Dörfern bettln, weil es in den Städten wenig Lebensmittelgeschäften gibt, oder sie haben nicht genug Zeug im Geschäft."

„Ja, im Krieg wurden fast alle Gebäude in den Städten, nicht nur Koblenz, ausbombardiert. Sogar die Läden die noch stehen, können ihren Vorrat nicht mehr wie vor dem Krieg bekommen. Deswegen sind Opa und aus Koblenz nach Macken gezogen."

„Ich bin froh, Oma, denn mir gefällt es hier. Jetzt verstehe ich auch die Milchkannen."

Die Verbindung zwischen Macken und der Aussenwelt wurde mir ein wenig klarer, aber ich wollte nicht oft an die Städte denken.

Perhaps it was the scarlet fever I had during the war when I was six, but my speech was very nasal. "Why are you talking through your nose. I can hardly understand you. Open your mouth!" Oma didn't mind, but my mother often interrupted me.

"I don't know, Mutti!" was always my answer. I just wasn't as perfect as she would have liked her own child to be. "Mutti, it's not my fault, and besides my ears are hurting too."

"Mother, what are we going to do with this child?" said my mother to Oma. "Marianne's ears have pus in them and her nose is always stopped up."

"Take her with you to Koblenz and have her examined by a doctor," Oma suggested. There were no doctors in Macken, but in Koblenz medical care had been reestablished after the war. Despite the terrible postwar economy, hospitals and doctors were already back in business.

"Mutti, I'm scared! What are they going to do with my nose?" I was reluctant to walk into the doctor's office.

A friendly doctor walked toward me. "We'll remove the adenoids from your nose, and then you will get your beautiful voice back," he tried to calm me down.

"Is it going to hurt?" I was shaking with fear.

"No, we're going to give you some medicine to make you go to sleep. When you wake up, you might feel a little pain, but two or

164

Vielleicht sprach ich immer durch die Nase wegen dem Scharlachfieber, „Warum sprichst du denn so aus der Nase? Mach doch den Mund auf!" Mutti fiel mir öfters ins Wort.

„Ich weiß nicht, Mutti!" war stets meine Antwort. Ich war eben nicht so perfekt, wie sie sich ihr eigenes Kind vorgestellt hatte. „Mutti, ich kann nichts dafür, mir tun auch die Ohren weh."

„Mutter, was machen wir mit dem Kind?" sprach Mutti meine Oma an. „Mariannes Ohren sind vereitert, und ihre Nase ist immer wie verstopft."

„Hol' sie doch mal nach Koblenz mit und laß sie mal von einem Artz untersuchen," schlug Oma vor. Es gab kein Arzt in Macken, aber in Koblenz gab es wieder Krankenpflege. Trotz der schrecklichen Nachkriegszeit, waren Krankenhäuser und Ärtze in den Städten wieder dienstbereit.

„Mutti, ich hab' Angst! Was machen sie mit meiner Nase?" Ich ging zögernd ins Sprechzimmer eines Arztes.

Ein freundlicher Arzt kam mir entgegen. „Wir holen die Polypen aus deiner Nase, dann wirst du deine schöne Stimme wiederbekommen." beruhigte er mich.

„Tut das denn weh?" Ich war schon am Zittern.

„Nein, wir geben dir ein Betäubunsmittel, dann schläfts du ein. Wenn du wieder wach wirst, fühlst du vielleicht Schmerzen, aber nach einem oder zwei Tage gehn die Schmerzen auch weg. Wir werden auch deine Ohren heilen."

three days later, all the pain will be gone. We're also going to heal your ears." They treated my ear infection with medicine, but my ears remained sensitive and prone to infection. This time I was only hospitalized for three days, and Mutti was allowed to visit me. I had successfully put the terror of my six weeks in the isolation ward three years earlier behind me. I actually enjoyed being taken care of and spoiled this time.

Three weeks later I was delivered back to my Oma in Macken.

My two girlfriends, Martha and Hiltrud sympathized with me for a few days, but soon they treated me normally again. We three had invented a wonderful game. We called our game "Hannele," because it was like Handeln (trading). We collected postage stamps, little pictures, and any papers that looked important. With our collections carefully stored in folders, we could amuse ourselves for hours and hours. Our game was especially fun on rainy days.

"Look here, I have a colorful Santa Claus," tempted Hiltrud. "Who will give me two postage stamps in exchange?"

Martha had no stamps, but she had a pretty holy card of the Madonna. "Marianne, if you will trade two postage stamps for this Madonna, then I can trade those with Hiltrud for the Santa Claus." We made the trade and all three of us were happy.

This is how we enjoyed many long winter evenings "trading."

166

Mit Medikamenten behandelte man meine Ohreninfektion, aber sie blieben sehr empfindlich und wurden leicht enzündet. Ich lag diesesmal nur drei Tage im Krankenhaus, und die Mutti durfte mich auch besuchen. Der Schreck meiner ersten Erfahrung vor drei Jahren, sechs Wochen mit Scharlachfieber auf der Isolierstation, hatte ich schon lange hinter mich gelegt.

Drei Wochen später wurde ich wieder in Macken abgeliefert.

Meine zwei Freundinnen, Martha und Hiltrud betrauerten mich paar Tage, aber ich wurde bald wieder als normal behandelt. Wir drei hatten ein wunderbares Spiel erfunden. Wir nannten das Spiel „Hannele," weil es wie Handeln war. Wir sammelten Bildchen, Briefmarken und andere Papiere. Mit unseren Sammlungen konnten wir uns beim Austausch und Bewundern stundenlang amüsieren. Das Spiel war besonders im Regenwetter ein wahres Vergnügen.

„Guck mal, ich habe einen bunten Nikolaus," lockte Hiltrud. „Wer gibt mir zwei schöne Briefmarken dafür?"

Martha hatte keine Briefmarken, aber sie hatte ein schönes Heiligenbildchen von der Muttergottes. „Marianne, wenn du mir zwei Briefmarken gibst, gebe ich dir dieses Heiligenbildchen, dann kann ich mir den Nikolaus anschaffen."

Abgebildet links: 1949 Meine Freundin Martha und ich. Martha war zwei Jahre älter.

Sometimes in the summer we used the cross bar of a wooden railing to do some tumbling. One time I was standing too close as Hiltrud took a turn. Her hard boot hit me on the forehead.

"Ouch! Hiltrud, you kicked me," I yelled and quickly put my hand up to my forehead. Three or four kids looked at me with scared faces.

Martha yelled, "Blood, blood! Your hand!" I took one look at my bloodied hand and started to scream. I screamed all the way home to convince myself I was still alive. I ran screaming into the house where my Oma tried to lay me on the couch so she could see what was wrong. I screamed so loud she couldn't get near me.

Suddenly she yelled right into my face, "Quiet! Hold still for a moment so I can check to see what's wrong!"

I stopped crying immediately. Oma washed my face and placed an adhesive bandage over the tiny wound. Soon I was ready to go back outside to play.

Oma always knew how to take care of my health issues. If I got a stomach ache, she gave me chamomile tea. When I missed my mother and got sad, Oma made waffles or her delicious split pea soup for me. She taught me how to knit and embroider. I was allowed to read her valued books, such as "Arabian Nights" or her set of encyclopedias. She let me stay in the house when I wasn't feeling well. I was allowed to build a castle with the kitchen chairs, or pretend to be a puppy. She let me play with other children outside or inside the house.

Manchmal im Sommer benutzten wir einen Zaun zum
Turnen. Der Zaun war ganz einfach: einige stehende Posten mit einer
waagerechten Stange. Einmal stand ich zu Nahe an der Stange als
Hiltrud sich darauf drehte. Ihr harter Bauernschuh traf meinen Kopf.

„Au ah! Hiltrud, du has mich getreten," rief ich und legte
meine Hand auf meine Stirn. Drei oder vier Kinder guckten mich
ängstlich an. Martha brüllte, „Blut! Blut! Deine Hand!" Ich nahm
einen Blick auf meine Hand die ganz blutig war und fing an zu
Schreien, um mich zu überzeugen, dass ich noch am Leben war. Ich
rannte schreiend ins Haus, wo meine Oma versuchte mich
hinzulegen. Ich schrie immer lauter. Oma konnte garnicht an mich
kommen, um mich zu behandeln.

Plötzlich brüllte sie mir direkt ins Gesicht, „Ruhe! Jetzt sei
doch mal still, und laß mich doch gucken was los ist!"

Mein Geschrei hörte sofort auf. Oma wusch mein Gesicht
und tat mir ein Pflaster auf die kleine Wunde. Dann durfte ich
wieder spielen gehen.

Oma wußte immer wie man mich wieder aufheitern konnte.
Wenn ich Bauchweh hatte, bekam ich Kamillentee. Wenn ich traurig
wurde und vermisste meine Mutti, machte mir Oma Waffeln oder
Erbsensuppe. Ich lernte stricken und durfte ihre wertvolle Bücher,
wie die Bibel, den Lexicon, oder sogar den "Tausend und Eine Nacht"
lesen. Ich durfte stundenlang im Haus bleiben und mit den
Küchenstühlen eine Burg bauen. Ich durfte mit anderen Kindern
draußen spielen, oder im Haus mit Hiltrud und Martha „Hannele."

Oma and Opa were my heroes. In their presence I was able to forget the outside world and the World War. Anything that somehow bothered or hurt me was chased away by my heroes.

"Oma, do you remember your grandparents?" I loved my grandparents so much, that I thought every child should feel the same comfort.

"Marianne, only one year after I was born, my Oma died. She was alread very old. My father told me about his parents, though. They lived in this same house, and there used to be a forge next to the barn."

"A forge? What's that?"

"That is a workshop where a blacksmith can work with iron. It has a very hot fire chamber and an anvil, and the smith can shape iron into horseshoes or other stuff," explained Oma.

"What happened to all that stuff?"

"After my grandfather was kicked by a horse, he died. My uncle Anton became the village smith, but my father never went back into the forge because he missed his father too much. The big grindstone in our backyard is still left over from that time. A few years later, Anton built a forge near his own house. My father tore down the old one and only ran his `Hospese Tavern` here."

"Your Opa got kicked by a horse?"

"Yes, that's what my father told me."

Oma und Opa waren meine Helden. Die Außenwelt und den Weltkrieg konnte ich in deren Gegenwart vergessen. Alles was mich irgendwie störte oder wehtat, wurde von meinen Helden weggejagt.

„Oma, kannst du dich an deine Großeltern erinnern?" Ich hatte meinen Opa und meine Oma so gern, daß ich dachte jedes Kind sollte diese Liebe spüren.

„Marianne, meine Oma war schon sehr alt, als ich auf die Welt kam. Sie starb, als ich nur ein Jahr alt war. Mein Vater hat mir von seinen Eltern erzählt. Sie haben im selben Haus gewohnt, aber früher hatten wir eine Schmiede neben der Scheune."

„Eine Schmiede? Was ist denn das?"

„Das ist eine Werkstatt mit einem großen Ofen und einem Amboß, wo ein Schmied mit Eisen arbeitet. Er kann dann Hufeisen und andere Sachen mit dem weichen Eisen formen," erklärte Oma.

„Was ist denn mit der Schmiede passiert?"

„Mein Großvater wurde von einem Pferd zu Tode getreten. Onkel Anton wurde dann der Dorfschmied. Er baute seine eigene Schmiede, und die Alte wurde abgerissen. Mein Vater ging nie mehr in die Schmiede, weil er seinen Vater zu sehr vermisste. Der große Schleifstein im Hof ist noch übriggeblieben.Mein Vater führte die `Hospese Wirtschaft' hier."

„Dein Opa wurde von einem Pferd getreten?"

„Ja, mein Vater hat mir davon erzählt."

A few months after my bump on the head my mother came to visit with an exciting piece of news.

"I've met a nice man in Frankfurt! He is in the American Air Force. He can even speak German because when he was a little child his parents emigrated to America and they spoke German to him." Mutti was more in love than I had ever seen before.

"You have my father. He is your husband," I murmured, quickly realizing that my cozy life was about to be changed.

"Marianne, you know that I don't get along with your father. I believe we will never become a real family. It's nobody's fault. It's just the way things are," my mother responded. Then she added, "We're getting a divorce." Oma and I just stared at her for a moment.

"Tilli, what kind of man is this American? Do you think you'll marry him and move to America?" Oma wanted to know. Suddenly, my mother's good mood disappeared.

"Mother, I don't know what will happen. At the moment times are so hard, food is so scarce and everything in Germany is so chaotic, that I can't even imagine the future. I'm just living from day to day. The man who treats me well, who loves me, and who does so much for me is the one I love. I really don't know whether I will ever marry him," my mother had become defensive.

Oma calmed down and started making coffee with the fresh coffee beans my mother had brought as a gift. A delicious cake on the

Paar Monate nach meinem kleinen Unfall am Kopf kam Mutti auf Besuch mit einer sehr erregenden Neuigkeit.

„Ich habe einen netten Mann in Frankfurt kennengelernt! Er ist bei der amerikanischen Militär, aber weil er als Kind nach Amerika aus Deutschland mit seinen Eltern auswanderte, kann er sogar deutsch sprechen." Mutti war ganz verliebt, wie ich sie noch nie sah.

„Du hast doch Vati. Er ist doch dein Mann," murmelte ich schnell auffassend, daß sich mein Leben etwa verändern könnte.

„Marianne, du weißt ja, daß ich mit deinem Vater nicht auskomme. Ich glaube wir werden nie eine richtige Familie. Es hat keiner die Schuld daran, es ist eben einfach so," erwiderte Mutti. „Wir lassen uns scheiden." Oma und ich waren verblüfft.

„Tilli, was ist der Amerikaner für ein Mann? Meinst du, du würdest ihn heiraten und nach Amerika auswandern?" wollte Oma wissen. Plötzlich war die gute Laune von Mutti weg.

„Mutter, ich weiß doch wirklich nicht was noch alles kommt. Im Moment sind die Zeiten so hart, das Lebensmittel so knapp, und alles in Deutschland so verwirrt, dass man sich garnicht die Zukunft vorstellen kann. Ich lebe nur von einem Tag zum Anderen. Den Mann, der mich lieb hat und mir viel guttut, werde ich lieben. Ob ich ihn wirklich heirate, weiß ich noch nicht." wehrte sich Mutti.

Oma beruhigte sich und fing an den guten Kaffee, der Mutti mitgebracht hatte, zu kochen. Ein prächtiger Streußelkuchen auf dem

decorated table brought the cozy atmosphere back into the kitchen. Soon all three of us were happy about Mutti's good luck.

"For Christmas, you'll be able to come to Frankfurt with me, Marianne. Then you'll get to know John. I'll come get you on December the twentieth," Mutti was all enthusiastic, but Oma's face went a little darker. She didn't say anything; after all, I was Mutti's child, not hers.

And that's how the years passed by in Macken. Now and then, back and forth, to Burgen or Koblenz or Frankfurt. After every move I could go back to Macken and recover from the stress until the next whim of my mother, but in 1949, my world turned upside down forever.

"Mother, John and I are married," declared my mother one day. "He has to go back to America in May, but I have to wait a while for my documents. I will probably get my visa and my permission to leave Germany in July."

Oma was devastated. "And what are you doing with Marianne?" I felt as if I had been transformed into a piece of furniture. What did they mean with 'what are you doing with Marianne?' It all seemed too rushed.

"Köves won't release Marianne to me. For now she will have to stay here because when we got divorced in 1947 we agreed to joint custody. First I have to come to an agreement with him, so that he'll give permission to let Marianne come to America."

geschmücktem Tisch brachte die gute Stimmung wieder zurück. Bald freuten wir uns alle über Muttis neue Glück.

„Zu Weihnachten darfst du nach Frankfurt kommen, Marianne. Dann wirst du John kennenlernen. Ich komme dich am zwanzigsten Dezember abholen." Mutti war begeistert, aber Omas Gesicht wurde ein wenig dunkler. Sie sagte aber nichts von Weihnachten oder ihrer Enttäuschung . Ich war ja letzten Endes Muttis Kind.

Und so vergingen die Jahre in Macken. Ab und zu, hin und her nach Burgen oder Koblenz oder Frankfurt. Ich konnte mich jedesmal in Macken von den Strapazen eines Umzugs bis zum nächsten Sprung meiner Mutter erholen, aber im April 1949 drehte sich meine Welt für ewig um.

„Mutter, John und ich sind verheiratet," deklarierte meine Mutti eines Tages. „Er muß schon im Mai zurück nach Amerika, aber ich muß auf meinen Paß mit dem Visa warten. Sehrwahrscheinlich bekomme ich ihn im Juli."

Oma war bestürzt. „Und was machst du mit Marianne?" Ich kam mir vor als ob ich in ein Stück Möbel verwandelt war. Was meinten sie mit ‚was machst du mit Marianne?' Alles kam mir schrecklich kalt und hastig vor.

„Der Köves läßt Marianne nicht los. Vorläufig muß sie noch hierbleiben weil wir ja in der Scheidung in 1947 ihre Betreuung geteilt haben. Erst muß ich noch mit ihm einig werden, daß er mir die Genehmigung Marianne nach Amerika kommen zu lassen gibt."

Whenever my mother was upset with my father, she called him Köves instead of Jakob. I didn't like this conversation between Oma and Mutti at all. I was twelve years old and loved my Oma and Opa way too much to get excited about leaving Germany and moving to America. What was in America for me? I didn't know one word of English! At the moment I was rendered speechless even in German. I was just a child, and my opinion didn't matter.

At the end of July my mother flew away. Now and then I got a letter or a package, but I was on edge the whole year. Mr. Zensen, my teacher, and Otto Andreas, the village priest, as well as my girlfriends, Hiltrud and Martha consoled me as much as they could.

"Oma, Oma! They've selected me to play the Christchild this year!" I was so excited that I almost fell up the stairs.

"What's the matter with you, Marianne? Who selected you?"

"My Catechism class voted. Usually, they pick a girl from the eighth grade, but this year they are making an exception. I'm only in the seventh grade."

Oma was surprised and gave me a big hug. "See, your school friends know that you've been very sad because your mother is in America. Your friends love you."

"Yes, Oma, that's what Martha told me."

Immer wenn Mutti mit meinem Vater unzufrieden war, nannte sie ihn Köves anstatt Jakob. Dieses Gespräch zwischen Oma und Mutti gefiel mir überhaupt nicht. Ich war zwölf Jahre alt und hatte meinen Opa und meine Oma viel zu lieb, um sie in Deutschland zu hinterlassen.

Was soll ich in Amerika? Ich konnte ja gar kein englisch! Im Moment wurde ich auch auf deutsch sprachlos. Ich war bloß ein Kind und durfte keine Meinung äussern.

Ende Juli flog Mutti weg. Ab und zu bekam ich Briefchen und Paketchen, aber ich blieb ein ganzes Jahr traurig. Lehrer Zinsen, Pfarrer Andreas und meine Freundinnen Hiltrud und Martha trösteten mich so viel sie konnten.

„Oma, Oma! Sie haben mich für's Christkindchen gewählt!" Ich war so aufgeregt, daß ich beinahe die Treppe ,raufgefallen wäre.

„Was ist denn los mit dir, Marianne? Wer hat dich gewählt?"

„Meine Katechismus Klasse. Oma, meistens wird ein Mädchen aus dem Achten Schuljahr gewählt, aber dieses Jahr machen sie eine Ausnahme."

Oma staunte. Sie drückte mich ganz fest. „Siehst Du, deine Schulkameraden wissen, daß du traurig bist, weil deine Mutti in Amerika ist. Deine Freundinnen haben dich sehr gern."

„Ja, Oma, das hat Martha auch gesagt.

"Now tell me calmly, what you're supposed to do as the Christchild."

"Just like every year, the Christchild, three angels and the Knight Ruprecht, will go through the whole village on Christmas Eve. We'll go in a group and knock on the doors of homes that have small children. They will invite us in, so we can give the children their Christmas plates of Marzipan, an apple and some nuts. Just think Oma, I always wished I could play the Christchild, and now I get my chance to do that."

"Marianne, what are you going to wear as a costume? It's always very cold in December."

"I'll be able to wear some warm clothes under the long white gown. First we're going to get ready at Rosenbach's. They have a chest full of costumes for Christmas, and they have enough room for us to get dressed. I'm going to have a long white gown, a veil and a crown, so the children won't recognize me."

"Then you'll have a lot of fun this Christmas even without your Mutti. Too bad that we don't have a camera. Next year, when you celebrate Christmas with your Mutti in America, you can tell her all about it," Oma made a very peculiar face.

"Oma, I want to be with my Mutti, but I don't want to leave you and Opa. Why can't we all live together anymore?" Suddenly I was very sad again.

„Jetzt erzähl' mir mal in aller Ruhe, was du als Christkindchen machen sollst."

„Oma, wie immer muss das Christkindchen mit drei Engelchen und dem Knecht Ruprecht am Heiligen Abend durch das Dorf wandern. Überall wo kleine Kinder wohnen, klopfen wir an. Dann wird die ganze Gruppe eingeladen, und wir geben kleine Gaben auf einem Weihnachtsteller, wie ein Stückchen Marzipan, einen Apfel, und paar Nüsse. Denk mal, Oma, dieses Jahr bin ich das Christkindchen! Das habe ich mir immer gewünscht."

„Marianne was ziehst du denn als Verkleidung an? Es ist im Dezember immer sehr kalt."

„Ich kann meine warmen Sachen unter dem langen weißen Kleid verstecken. Wir gehen zuerst zu Rosenbach's. Die haben eine Kiste voll Weihnachtskleidung. Da haben wir auch genug Platz uns zu verkleiden. Ich bekomme ein langes weißes Kleid, eine Krone und einen Schleier, daß die Kinder mich nicht erkennen."

„Dann wirst du dieses Jahr auch ohne deine Mutti viel Spaß an Weihnachten haben. Schade, daß wir keinen Photoapparat haben. Du kannst ihr ja nächstes Jahr, als du in Amerika Weihnachten mit deiner Mutti feierst, vom Christkindchen erzählen," Oma machte wieder ein ganz komisches Gesicht.

„Oma, ich will bei meiner Mutti sein, aber ich will nicht so weit weg von dir und Opa sein. Warum können wir nicht alle zusammen leben?" Plötzlich wurde ich wieder ganz traurig.

Opa sympathized with me, but Oma couldn't hide her pain. We began to fight about every little thing. After Christmas we screamed almost every day at each other, knowing that both of us would rather be screaming at someone else.

Suddenly we got the news that my father had signed the paperwork for my emigration. He gave his consent under the condition that I would travel by ship rather than by airplane. My passport and my ticket arrived in plenty of time. My clothing was packed. Dreamlike, I prepared myself for the impending adventure. In November 1950, I was supposed to travel in the company of an officially appointed married couple. At the last moment the couple had their documents revoked. They apparently hadn't been properly denazified yet, so their travel was denied. Despite my youth, I was allowed to travel on my own into the wide world.

My time in Macken was finished.

Opa hatte Mitleid mit mir, aber Oma konnte ihren Schmerz nicht verheimlichen. Nach Weihnachten fingen wir an, uns um jede Kleinigkeit zu streiten. Fast jeden Tag schrieben wir uns gegenseitig in dem Bewußtsein an, daß wir Beide lieber jemand anders anschreihen würden.

Plötzlich hieß es mein Vater hätte die Genehmigung zu meiner Auswanderung unter der Bedingung, daß ich per Schiff anstatt Flugzeug reise, gegeben. Mein Paß und meine Reisekarte kamen rechtzeitig an. Man besorgte sich um meine Kleidung. Traumhaft bereitete ich mich auf das vorliegende Abenteuer. Im November 1950 sollte ich in der Begleitung einem fremden aber amtlich ausgesuchten Ehepaar auswandern. Im letzten Moment durfte das Ehepaar nicht verreisen, weil die Beiden noch nicht denazifiert waren. Trotz meiner Jugend genehmigte man mir allein in die Weltgeschichte zu reisen.

Meine Zeit in Macken war vorüber.

. 1947 Maria und Hans Küppers (Oma and Opa) with Marianne

Einige Familienbilder

. 1967 hinten, Martha, Magda, Maria (Oma) Lili,
Valentin, vorne, Karin, Leni, Gabi

. 1956 Maria Küppers (my Oma) and Tilli Miller, nee Küppers visit the grave of my Opa, Hans Küppers in Macken

. 1952 Martha Pons, nee Hammes with her two children, Lili and Bernd

. 1955 Martha, Maria mit Baby Karin

Epilog

And so, I'm in awe of the women who have given me the opportunity to enjoy life in California. Maria Korzilius, my great-great-grandmother, suffered the loss of several children without losing heart. Her one surviving son, Moritz, married Barbara Pies, a pretty girl from a neighboring village. I didn't have the opportunity to meet them, but their youngest child, Maria Hammes (Oma) became my grandmother and role model. Maria and her four children survived World War I, the Inflation, the Depression, World War II and the Aftermath of WWII in Germany. My mother, Mathilde Maria (Tilli) was born prematurely and suffered many illnesses throughout her life, yet she demonstrated the courage and strength of her female ancestors. Despite her misgivings about starting life with a different husband in a different country in a different language, she left Germany in 1949 without me. With great difficulty she succeeded in convincing my father to let me join her in America where I would have opportunites only imagined a hundred and fifty years earlier by my hero, Maria Korzilius.

Nachwort

Und so kann ich nur über die Frauen, die mir mein jetziges Leben in Kalifornien schenkten, staunen. Maria Korzilius, die Grossmutter meiner Grossmutter verlor sechs ihrer Kinder ohne den Mut zu verlieren. Ihr einziger überlebender Sohn, Moritz, heiratete Barbara Pies aus Dommershausen, ein Nachbarsdorf. Ich habe sie nie kennengelernt, aber ihre jüngste Tochter, Maria Hammes (Oma) wurde meine Grossmutter. Maria und ihre vier Kinder überlebten manches Unheil, wie der Erste Weltkrieg, die Inflation, der Zweite Weltkrieg, und das Elend der Nachkriegszeit.

Meine Mutter, Mathilde Maria (Tilli) wurde frühzeitig geboren und litt viele Krankheiten, aber doch bewies sie die Energie und Tapferkeit ihrer Vorfahren. Trotz ihrer Angst ein neues Leben in einem fremden Land mit einer fremden Sprache anzufangen, flog sie mutig ohne mich aus Deutschland. Mit allem Ach und Krach überzeugte sie meinen Vater, dass ich in Amerika Gelegenheiten finden würde, wovon meine Vorfahren nur träumen konnten. Vor hundert fünfzig Jahren hatte meine Heldin, Maria Korzilius, ihrem Sohn dieses Ergebnis vorausgesagt.

1964 Die 4 Generationen in Kalifornien. Marianne, Maria, Tilli mit Vivienne, Kathryn und Elizabeth

Just a few more Words

Many years earlier. when Maria Korzilius, her stepdaughter Liz, and the midwife Lucille, foretold Moritz's future in the kitchen, they had no way of knowing how true their words were. They told him about a wide world, that they themselves knew nothing about. They only knew that times could change very rapidly. The Industrial Revolution was in full swing. Maria knew that her family would be affected sooner or later.

The adult children of Moritz moved to the cities, where they could establish new families and earn larger fortunes. Perhaps they could eventually even start new lives in foreign lands.

The family of Moritz has, indeed, spread across the world.

His oldest daughter was Magdalene. Her great-granddaughter is currently living and working in Washington, D. C.

His third daughter was Barbara, whose two daughters emigrated to the United States before World War II because they had married Jewish men.

His sons remained in Germany, but the oldest one, Peter lived and worked in East Germany behind the Iron Curtain.

His youngest daughter, Maria, was affected the most. Two of her three daughters emigrated to America after the Second World War. Her granddaughter Marianne married an American of Chinese ancestry.

Noch einen kleinen Anhang

Als damals Maria Korzilius, ihre Stieftochter Liz, und die Hebamme Luzille die Zukunft Moritzs in der Küche voraussagten, konnten sie nicht wissen wie echt ihre Worte waren. Sie erzählten ihm von einer grossen Welt die sie selbst nicht kannten, aber sie wussten, daß die Zeiten sich schnell verändern könnten. Die Industrielle Revolution war schon im Gange. Maria wusste schon, dass ihre Familie auch damit verbunden war.

Die Kinder des erwaschsenen Moritz zogen in die Städte, ihre eigenen Familien und Vermögen gründen, und eventuell sogar in fernen Ländern ein neues Leben anfangen.

Die Familie des Moritz hat sich wirklich über die Welt verbreitet.

Seine älteste Tochter war Magdalene, dessen Urenkelin zur Zeit in Washington, D.C. wohnt und arbeitet.

Seine dritte Tochter war Barbara, dessen zwei Töchter schon vor dem Zweiten Weltkrieg nach Amerika auswanderten, weil sie Juden geheiratet hatten.

Seine Söhne blieben in Deutschland, aber der älteste, Peter, wohnte in Ostdeutschland hinter dem Eisernen Vorhang.

Moritz' jüngste Tochter, Maria,wurde am Meisten betroffen. Zwei ihrer Töchter und eine Enkelin wanderten nach dem Zweiten Weltkrieg nach Amerika aus.

Maria's oldest daughter, Martha, lived in Trier, where her three children and one grandson still reside. Her younger grandson studied foreign languages at the University and is employed with the German Embassy. He was sent to Greece for a few years before he was transferred to China. There he met his wife of Chinese ancestry.

Martha's older grandson came to visit Marianne in California for a few weeks when he was only nineteen years old. After he got married in Trier several years later, his sister-in-law also spent some time with Marianne's family. When Marianne discovered that his daughter was an exchange student in Vancouver, British Columbia in Canada, she invited her to San Francisco, Disneyland and Las Vegas. A year later both families met in Vancouver, Canada for a visit.

And so, it can be truly said, "Maria's posterity is spread all over the world. Maria lives!"

. 1965 Magda, Gabi, Maria & Jupp Küppers in Deutschland

Ihre Enkelin, Marianne heiratete einen amerikanischen Mann chinesischer Abstammung.

Martha, die älteste Tochter Marias, wohnte später in Trier, wo ihre drei Kinder und ein Enkel immernoch wohnen. Ihr jüngster Enkel lernte Fremdsprachen auf der Universität und wurde bei der deutschen Botschaft in Griechenland angestellt. Nach paar Jahren dort, wurde er nach China versetzt, wo er seine Frau chinesischer Abstammung kennenlernte.

Marthas älterer Enkel kam nach Kalifornien als er nur neunzehn Jahre alt war, um Marianne kurz zu besuchen. Nachdem er sich paar Jahre später in Trier verheiratete, kam seine Schwägerin auch auf Besuch. Plötzlich erfuhr Marianne, daß seine Tochter Austauschstudent in Vancouver, British Columbia in Kanada ist. Marianne und ihr Mann zeigten dem Mädchen San Francisco, Disneyland und Las Vegas. Ein Jahr später besuchten sie die ganze Familie in Vancouver.

Und so, kann man wahrhaftig sagen, „Der Nachwuchs Marias ist auf der ganzen Welt verbreitet. Maria lebt!"

A few more family pictures- Noch einige Familienbilder

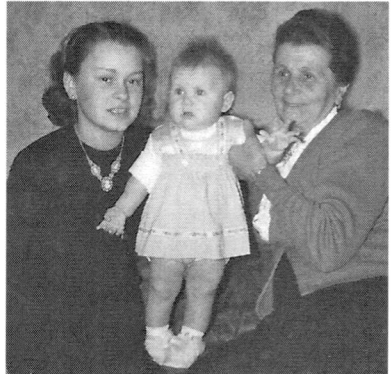

1953 Oma mit Lili & Gabi

. 1960 Martha, Oma, Mutti & Karin

. 1950's Ketta and Marlene Dott

1968 Maria, hier 80 Jahre alt, landet in Los Angeles. Ihre Töchter, Leni & Tilli holen Maria am Flughafen ab.

Maria, 80 years old in this picture, arrives in Los Angeles. Her daughters, Leni and Tilli are there to pick her up.

. 1974 Geschwister (siblings) Leni, Jupp, Tilli & Martha in California, USA

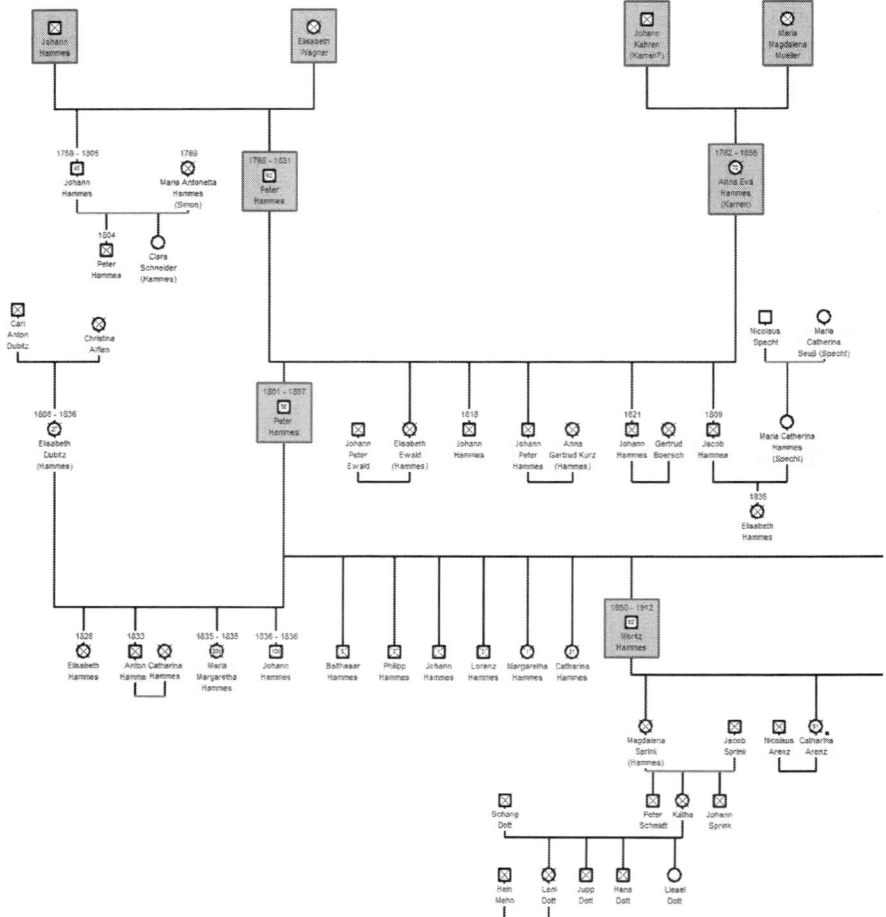

The author, Marianne Tong, has represented the family tree using the Genopro.com program. The family tree can be accessed on the Internet, but it is passworded.

Family members may contact the author at **marianne.tong@gmail.com** *to request the login information.*

194

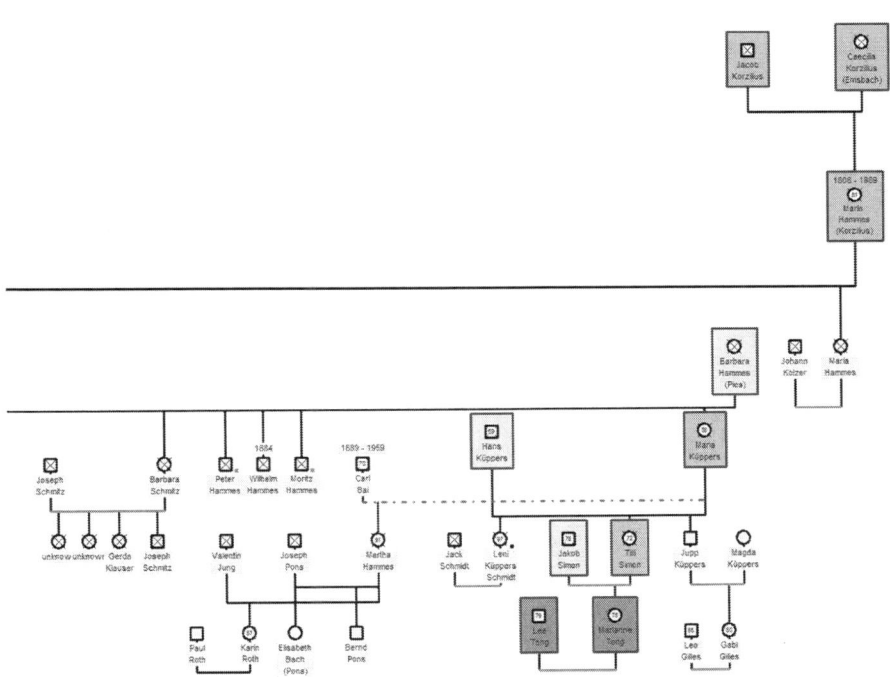

Marianne Tong hat den Stammbaum mit dem Genopro.com Program hergestellt. Der Stammbaum ist am Internet erreichbar, aber nur mit einem Kennwort.

Mitglieder der Familie mögen sich mit Marianne in Verbindung setzen um die LOGIN information zu erbitten.
marianne.tong@gmail.com

About the Author

Marianne was a healthy little German girl until the ravages of World War II took their toll. She barely survived terrorizing air raids, a six weeks hospital stay on an isolation ward, escape into the Alps, and her parents' divorce.

When her mother married an American and emigrated from Germany to America, Marianne was expected to follow, leaving many loved ones and her heritage behind. Her unaccompanied ocean voyage from Italy to New York changed her life into that of a normal American teenager.

In a twist of fate, Marianne met a Los Angeles-born Chinese American serviceman in Bermuda, causing a great uproar in her family.

*Eventually they got married and raised four children while remaining active in a variety of community events, including earning University degrees. Marianne's Memoir **The Little Girl That Could**, was published in 2009.*

*Marianne's desire to learn about her ancestry has led her to discover precious information in documents from Germany. Her curiosity about her husband's ancestry led her to do research at the National Archives & Records Administration in San Bruno. Among the aged files from Angel Island, she has found a wealth of materials to weave the tales in **Mindpieces,** a Collection of Short Works, published in 2011.*

Über die Schriftstellerin

Marianne war ein kräftiges deutsches Mädchen in Koblenz bis die verheerenden Auswirkungen des Zweiten Weltkriegs sie fast zu Grunde brachten.

Als ihre Mutter sich scheiden ließ und einen Amerikaner heiratete, sollte Marianne trotz der herzzerreißender Trennung von der beliebten Oma ihr folgen. Die unbegleitete Seereise mit dreizehn Jahren wandelte das Kind Marianne in eine junge Amerikanerin.

Das Schicksal brachte Marianne nach Bermuda, who sie ihren Mann von chinesischer Abstammung kennenlernte. Die Familie, und besonders Mariannes Stiefvater John, kam deshalb in einen Aufruhr.

*Trotz dem Widerstand, heiraten Marianne und Lee. Sie gründeten eine Familie mit vier Kindern. Die Geschichte der zwei ist in Mariannes Memoir, **„The Little Girl That Could"** in 2009 herausgegeben.*

*Marianne hatte immer den Wunsch mehr über ihre eigene Herkunft, so wie die ihres Mannes, zu erforschen. Dieser Wunsch trieb sie zur Entdeckung von alten Akten in NARA „National Archives and Records Administration" in San Bruno, Kalifornien. Was da gefunden wurde, musste auch in Geschichten verwandelt werden, die jetzt in einem Buch, **„Mindpieces"** herausgegeben sind.*

Every summer from 1985 to 1995, at least three times a week, Marianne educated and entertained her grandchildren in her home.

In her book, **_Banking, Bowling & Beethoven_**, *Marianne describes the ten summers of fun she devoted to her grandchildren with sports, music and money management.*

Marianne and her husband Lee make their home in northern California within easy driving distance of their children, grandchildren, great-grandchildren and their extended family.

Von 1985 bis 1995, als Mariannes Enkelkinder aufwuchsen, führte sie in ihrem Heim eine Familiensommerschule mit Musik, Sport und finanziellem Unterricht mindestens dreimal in der Woche,.

*In ihrem Buch, „**Banking, Bowling & Beethoven**" beschreibt Marianne diesen Sommerferienspaß mit ihren Enkelkindern.*

Marianne und Lee Tong machen ihr Heim im Norden von Kalifornien, nicht weit entfernt von ihren Kindern, Enkel und Urenkel.

Made in the USA
San Bernardino, CA
13 June 2013